Export-Import

Export Import

JOSEPH A. ZODL

BETTERWAY BOOKS

Cincinnati, Ohio

If you would like information on Joseph Zodl's classes and seminars, please write to:

Joseph Zodl Seminars
PO Box 20232
Phoenix, AZ 85036

The forms on pages 65, 74, 76, 77, 81, 82, 83, 85 and 87 are reprinted with permission of Unz & Co.
190 Baldwin Avenue
Jersey City, NJ 07306

99 98 97 96 95   5 4 3 2 1

Library of Congress Cataloging-in-Publication Data

Zodl, Joseph A.
    Export-import / Joseph A. Zodl.—2nd ed.
        p.   cm.
    Includes index.
    ISBN 1-55870-388-8
    1. Export marketing—United States. I. Title.
HF1416.5.Z63   1995
658.8'48—dc20   95-3449
                                                                          CIP

Edited by Perri Weinberg-Schenker
Designed by Brian Roeth

To my vendors and associates, clients, customers and students.

ACKNOWLEDGMENTS

Let me express my special thanks to Jill Barshop, Judy Mata, Felipe Reyes, Don Snyder and Frank Woods for their invaluable help and suggestions in writing this book.

CONTENTS

INTRODUCTION

If you're in business, either you or your competitors are in international business. The world market is growing smaller every day. And I am optimistic that as it continues to shrink, it will draw more and more American businesses into the arena of world trade.

When I wrote the first edition of this book in 1992, it was in response to inquiries from people looking for a book outlining how best to get started in international trade, particularly in exporting. I found that the books on the market were either (1) designed for very large businesses involved in franchising, opening their own offices overseas and the like, or (2) economics textbooks dealing with the balance of payments, foreign investment, and so on.

I wrote this book with the intention of giving you many of the answers you need to enter into international trade and pointing you to knowledgeable sources for the other answers. The book is geared to the small- to medium-sized company wanting to get involved in exporting or importing products right away, with a minimum of complications.

This revised edition continues to provide you with the answers to your crucial questions, but it also has been expanded to provide you with all kinds of current information that will factor into your business decisions: information on The North American Free Trade Agreement, important new federal programs, and the constantly changing import procedures.

I have been involved in international trade since 1978 on both the export and import sides and, more recently, as a consultant and college teacher. My position has always been this: The problem is not that we import too much—it's that we don't export enough. Quality imports increase our standard of living; quality exports enable us to pay for it. In a healthy economy, exporting and importing go hand in hand.

This book will show you how to join in.

Joseph Zodl
Phoenix, Arizona, U.S.A.
April 20, 1995

Why You Should Be Exporting or Importing

Many people in the United States wonder how "important" it is for their company to become involved in world trade. The answer is: extremely important.

I emphasize "people in the United States" because people in many other countries take quite naturally to the idea that if they are in business, they are part of the world economy and must think in terms of export and import for their business to prosper. Business people in Japan, Hong Kong, Germany, and other of our leading international trading partners have never thought of themselves as anything less than active participants in a world economy.

With our large domestic market and our very large domestic industry, the United States has for years been able to do quite well with many of its business people, particularly small-business owners, letting international business pass them by.

EXPLORING THE WORLD AS YOUR MARKET

Today we are beginning to realize that the firm that isn't thinking in terms of international trade should start thinking about going out of business. Our economy is global, and you must be part of that global economy for your business to prosper. Our consumers and our industry can no longer be insulated by national borders.

You have taken an important step by buying a book on international business. Many people are so convinced that entering the international marketplace is too difficult that they never ask the right questions or take any action at all. So you and I are in agreement that world trade is something for your firm to get involved in, and profitably.

Is it too difficult to become involved in world trade and make a profit doing it? The short answer is no, it is not difficult. But how does one learn enough to get into world trade efficiently and make a profit? No one knows it all. Whole libraries have been written about world trade. The purpose of this one volume is to show you:

1. The basic concepts of international business from the point of view of a U.S.-based exporter and/or importer operating a small- to medium-sized business dealing in U.S. dollars rather than foreign currencies.
2. The vocabulary and terminology.
3. Where to go for help.

After you have finished this book, you should be able to become involved very quickly and know exactly what you are doing as you are doing it. From the feedback I've received from clients over the years, I guarantee that you will know more about exporting and importing than some of the people who are already doing it and making a profit at it.

This book takes a basic approach to international trade. I assume that you are not ready to open branches overseas, franchise in foreign countries, or hire your own salespeople in each country. Therefore, to uncomplicate matters, I have excluded a great deal of material from the world of "international trade."

Learn Just What You Need

All you need to get started exporting or importing is to know your own business and to become acquainted with the basic information in this book.

You, as an exporter, make a product in the United States, sell it overseas, make your shipment, and get paid for it in U.S. dollars. Or perhaps you act as a middle agent, buying a product someone else makes and reselling it at a profit to an overseas customer for U.S. dollars.

Or you, as an importer, locate a product overseas and import it for sale domestically, either as a wholesale distributor or direct to end users through your own retail business. Still, you deal in U.S. dollars.

Whether you are exporting or importing, you do not have to worry about the exchange rates of foreign currencies because you are going to buy and sell only in U.S. dollars (for now—you can always get into foreign currencies at some future date, although I do not particularly recommend it).

If you are exporting, you do not have to worry about foreign tax laws or employment regulations because you are not setting up a factory there. You do not have to worry about Value Added Tax (VAT) in Europe because the wholesale customer to whom you are selling will be used to taking care of that. You do not have to get involved in preparing your advertising in foreign languages except to help your customer as he prepares the advertising he will use in his country. (Send samples of ads that have worked in the United States that he can adapt and then have translated.)

KNOW YOUR PRODUCT

So you can get into export and import the easy way: by sticking to your business—the business and products you already know. Your business—whether it is paper clips or solar technology—remains your business. All that changes is your scope: your marketing territory (as an exporter) or your prospective worldwide vendors (as an importer).

If you are considering getting into international trade with a side business and a completely new product, let me caution you that the product must still be one you know a good deal about. Would you go to an antique auction, or a stamp or coin auction, or deal in commodity futures without

knowing something about them? Would you even look at a used car without having some idea of the book value? Just as in these situations, in international trade you have to have the knowledge.

Knowing your product is the first rule of any business. As you enter the international trade arena you need to stay in that business and let the experts in shipping, banking, customs law and other areas guide you through.

The second rule should be to ask the experts before you begin a transaction. Get all the information you can on prices, commodities, shipping weights, etc., and then get expert guidance before committing yourself.

PRODUCT KNOWLEDGE

If I opened a restaurant, I would be out of business in ninety days for the simplest reason: I don't know anything about running a restaurant; I have never even worked in one. So I would probably make every possible—and expensive—mistake.

One of the keys in any business—and certainly in international trade—is to stick with what you know. If something new appeals to you, get to know it first before you spend any money.

Licensing

For most commodities, you can export freely under what is termed a "general license." The general license means that you can export the goods without obtaining a specific "validated" license from the U.S. government.

Starting with a book called the *Export Administration Regulations*, published by the U.S. Commerce Department, you determine if a license is needed for a particular transaction. If a validated license is not required, then you can export freely without any government licensing.

Fundamentally, goods needing a validated license are:

- Weapons
- High-tech products that can be used against the United States or its allies
- Goods in short supply in the United States, possibly strategic goods, that are restricted, perhaps on a temporary basis.

To obtain export licenses in these cases, contact the U.S. Department of Commerce, U.S. and Foreign Commercial Service, with offices in most large cities. They will help you determine if export licensing is needed and assist you with the application.

Import licensing is generally needed only for goods that you need a license to handle anyway: drugs, weapons and alcoholic beverages. To import these products you need the same licenses required by the regulatory agencies of the state or federal government as anyone handling the commodity.

For certain countries with which the United States is not on friendly terms, there are special licensing procedures. These countries currently include Cambodia, Cuba, Iran, Iraq, Libya and North Korea. You are not likely to be involved with these countries.

TARGETING YOUR MARKETS

What countries should you target for your international trade efforts? Companies in countries that are the United States's best customers are your best prospects. They like U.S. products now and will probably import more from us in the years to come. Your best possible sources for products are the countries that are already the United States's best sources. They know our tastes, needs and wants and can accommodate them. Of course, you can work with other

countries, too, and probably will.

Who are our major trading partners? Do you know:

- What country sells the most to the United States? That is, from what country do we import the most?
- What country is our best customer? That is, to what country do we sell the most?

You will find out the answers shortly, along with the most recent statistics for our top trading partners in both export and import. You will be impressed with the possibilities.

THE ADVANTAGES TO EXPORTING

Besides the basic profit motive, there are two other major reasons for exporting.

1. It takes some of the peaks and valleys out of the business cycle. One country may have an economic downturn while another country is enjoying relative prosperity. With customers in the United States and several other countries simultaneously, you'll be able to maintain more consistent business projections from year to year.

2. It postpones the end of the product cycle. By the time a U.S. market for a product is saturated, the product can be introduced in new countries.

DIRECT AND INDIRECT EXPORTING

Many companies, possibly including some of your competitors, are making money by exporting indirectly. This can involve selling a product to a company that uses it in making a more finished product (machine parts to a machinery exporter, for example), who then has export accounts as well as domestic accounts. In fact, your product may already be exported as part of a larger product without your knowing it. There is nothing wrong with being in the indirect market, but if your product is good enough that it can meet specifications of buyers around the world, you should consider exporting it directly as well.

Export Trading Companies

Some companies work with Export Trading Companies (ETCs). These companies buy products for resale overseas. Japan has been using this process for years, and you know the names of many of their largest trading companies, or "sogoshosha"—Matsushita, Mitsubishi, Mitsui, Sumitomo, Toshiba. The concept has not resulted in as many large Export Trading Companies in the United States as there are in Japan, but there are many, many small ones. (One quite large ETC in the United States is The Getz Corporation, 640 Sacramento Street, San Francisco, CA 94111.) Check your local yellow pages for a list. Also, the U.S. Department of Commerce is an excellent source for finding ETCs.

Export Management Companies

Export Management Companies (EMCs) are another alternative. These companies seek to represent your product overseas, but instead of buying it from you and reselling it, they put a sale together and then look to you for a commission. They ask the importer to open a letter of credit that calls for, say, 90 percent of the invoice amount to be paid to you after shipment and 10 percent to be paid to them. Export Management Companies can be found in the yellow pages and through the U.S. Department of Commerce.

YOUR SOURCE FOR FINDING PRODUCTS

If you choose to be a middle agent, buying U.S. products for resale abroad (Export Trading Company) or collecting a commission on your sales (Export Management Company), one of your best sources for products is the Thomas Register of Industrial Corporations.

This lists manufacturers of products by product classification, including names, addresses, telephone and fax numbers and contact names. It should be available at your public library. The publisher is Thomas International Publishing Co., 1 Penn Plaza, 250 West 34 Street, New York, NY 10119.

A SIMPLE TRANSACTION

The following sample details a straightforward domestic transaction. Would you have difficulties completing it?

1. A prospective customer in Brownsville, Texas, asks you for a quotation on 1,000 pieces of your product, let's say books, to be delivered to his warehouse in Brownsville.
2. You price out your product on the basis of $10 per book wholesale, for a total of $10,000.
3. The books are packed 100 to a carton, 100 pounds per carton, for a total of 10 cartons weighing 1,000 pounds altogether.
4. Next, you call a trucker who serves both your city and Brownsville, Texas, and ask for a rate quotation for 1,000 pounds of books. The quotation is $17 per 100 pounds, for a total of $170.
5. You quote your customer $10,170 delivered to Brownsville ($10,000 + $170).
6. He sends you a check for $10,170.
7. You ship to the customer.
8. Order complete.

This is a simple domestic order—a customer asks you to ship direct to him, prepay the freight, and add it onto his invoice. And in this case, the customer is not asking for credit, but is sending a check before you ship. This is an easy order to handle, and a prepaid order means no credit or collection problems.

Would you believe that many business people all over the United States ship to customers in Mexico just that way? A Mexican buyer asks for a quotation for your goods, shipped truck-prepaid to Brownsville, Texas; Nogales, Arizona or some other border point. He sends you a check drawn in U.S. dollars on a U.S. bank in a major U.S. city. You simply ship to the border point, where his Customs Broker, paid by him, arranges customs clearance and shipment into Mexico.

It could not be easier. It is the same as the easiest domestic transaction. People are doing it every day.

Many companies ship to customers in the Caribbean and other points in the western hemisphere on the same basis, shipping truck-prepaid to Miami, Florida, and collecting the money in advance.

Some U.S. companies sell to Japan by shipping to a Freight Forwarder in Los Angeles or San Francisco that consolidates many smaller shipments into one large shipment for ocean transportation to a Japanese customer. Others sell to European customers, who ask that the goods be shipped to New York for consolidation with their other purchases.

There are many variations on the above. I'll tell you more about Customs Brokers, Freight Forwarders and Consolidators in later chapters. And, of course, not all customers want to prepay; I'll talk about letters of credit and other alternatives as well.

But this simplest of transactions, prepaid and shipped to a point within the United States, is a transaction that many companies around the United States—perhaps including some of your competitors—are undertaking on a regular basis, knowing far less about world trade than you will know even at the end of this chapter.

THE MAGIC FORMULA FOR EXPORTING

Some people hesitate to get involved in international trade because they fear shipping an order overseas and never getting paid for it.

Let me introduce you to my "Magic Formula for Exporting." Follow it in this sequence to protect yourself and ensure your export business is successful.

1. *Get the order (you don't have anything to worry about up to that point).*
2. *Make sure you are going to get paid for the order (more about that in Chapter seven).*
3. *Ship the order.*

OUR BIGGEST CUSTOMER

I asked earlier if you knew who our number-one trading partners are for import and export. As you can see from the Department of Commerce lists on page 9, the answer to both is Canada.

People don't always think of Canada as our best customer, but Canada sells us more goods than does any other country.

And Canada, always one of the easiest countries for U.S. companies to buy from and sell to, is even easier to work with now under The North American Free Trade Agreement (NAFTA).

Almost everyone is surprised by Japan's position on the list. Folks who thought that Japan was our biggest supplier are surprised to see them as our second biggest, and almost everyone is amazed to see that Japan is our second biggest customer. We sell everything from food products to raw materials to manufactured goods at the rate of more than one hundred million dollars worth a day! In fact, Japan buys more goods per capita from the United States ($391) than the United States buys per capita from Japan ($374).

Our balance of payments problem with Japan is not that we import too much from Japan, but that we export too little to Japan. While this is partly a political problem, the fact is that many U.S. companies are exporting to Japan and making large profits right now.

Our third largest trading partner is Mexico, and there we run a healthy trade surplus. U.S. products are very popular throughout Mexico, and it's an excellent market for a U.S. exporter.

Note that two of our top three trading partners are our partners in NAFTA. Canada, Mexico and the United States form the world's largest free trade area, and trade among them can only increase in the years to come.

LANGUAGE AND CULTURE

Some people raise the question of foreign languages. The language of international business is English. You can send letters and brochures in English to virtually every country in the world and receive your replies in English, including your financial documentation.

I do not minimize, of course, the effectiveness of knowing even a little of the other person's language, and I encourage you to pursue any interest you may have in foreign languages. My point is that you do not have to become multilingual to get started in international trade any more than you need to hire a computer programmer to use a PC.

When you need translation services (and the need will come about some day), you can find translators in the yellow pages who will be able to handle any document or even a personal visit from your foreign customer.

AT&T even has an on-line interpreter service available, called "Language Line" (see Resource List at the back of the book).

Many people ask about foreign cultures and customs. For example:

- Is it considered impolite to sit so that the sole of your shoe faces an Arab person?
- Is it considered impolite in some countries, even obscene, to give the "A-OK" sign of thumb-meeting-index-finger, with the three remaining fingers extended?
- In giving a gift to a Latin American associate, is it considered impolite to give handkerchiefs, implying that you wish the recipient hardship?

The answer to each of these questions is *yes*. But let's put the culture issue in perspective right here:

1. When business is conducted by fax, letter and even telephone, the cross-cultural conflicts are minimal, if they exist at all. This will be most of your communication in starting out.

2. When people from different cultures do meet, and are trying to get along, they tend to understand that each other's culture is different and to make allowances. Here I speak of a personal contact at a trade show, or a brief visit to each other's place of business. These contacts would be your next step.

3. For an extended contact, such as a stay of several weeks as a guest of your associate (or if your associate were to visit you for several weeks), or if you were fortunate enough to accept an employment contract that would keep you in a foreign country for several months or even years, the situation would change.

LEADING U.S. SUPPLIERS U.S. GENERAL MERCHANDISE IMPORTS, 1993 (CUSTOMS VALUE)	
	$BILLIONS
1. Canada	110.9
2. Japan	107.3
3. Mexico	39.9
4. China	31.5
5. Germany	28.6
6. Taiwan	25.1
7. United Kingdom	21.7
8. South Korea	17.1
9. France	15.2
10. Italy	13.2
11. Singapore	12.8
12. Malaysia	10.6
13. Hong Kong	9.6
14. Thailand	8.5
15. Venezuela	8.1
16. Saudi Arabia	7.7
17. Brazil	7.5
18. Switzerland	6.0
19. Netherlands	5.5
20. Indonesia	5.4
21. Belgium-Luxembourg	5.4
22. Nigeria	5.3
23. Philippines	4.9
24. India	4.6
25. Sweden	4.5

Source: U.S. Dept. of Commerce

TOP 25 U.S. MARKETS U.S. DOMESTIC AND FOREIGN GOODS EXPORTS, 1993 (F.A.S. VALUE)	
	$BILLIONS
1. Canada	100.2
2. Japan	48.0
3. Mexico	41.6
4. United Kingdom	26.4
5. Germany	19.0
6. Taiwan	16.3
7. South Korea	14.8
8. France	13.3
9. Netherlands	12.8
10. Singapore	11.7
11. Hong Kong	9.9
12. Belgium-Luxembourg	9.4
13. China	8.8
14. Australia	8.3
15. Switzerland	6.8
16. Saudi Arabia	6.7
17. Italy	6.5
18. Malaysia	6.1
19. Brazil	6.0
20. Venezuela	4.6
21. Israel	4.4
22. Spain	4.2
23. Argentina	3.8
24. Thailand	3.8
25. Philippines	3.5

Source: U.S. Dept. of Commerce

You would find it worthwhile to invest time and money in a class on that nation's culture so you could fit into the new culture as much as possible. At that stage, you would invest in learning the language anyway, wouldn't you?

People do make allowances for foreign visitors making mistakes due to linguistic and cultural differences. For U.S.-based exporters and importers, the problems are minimal because most contacts are in cate-

gories 1 and 2. When situations do come up, you will deal with them easily. The important points, I have found, are:

- Talk as politely as you would to your most sensitive U.S. customer, and a little more slowly.
- Avoid gestures. That is where misunderstandings most easily take place.

Ethnocentrism

Sociologists use the word *ethnocentrism* to describe an assumption that the way you do things in your culture is the way it should be done everywhere. Anyone who does otherwise is simply incorrect.

For example, many European hotels include breakfast in the price of a room. So it may come as a shock to Europeans visiting the United States to have to pay extra for breakfast. Their shock would be an ethnocentric response.

Watch out for your own ethnocentric tendencies. Each society is used to its own way and considers other ways strange, yet cultural differences are one of the things that makes traveling outside your own country so fascinating.

THE INTERNATIONAL LANGUAGE

For a time, there was an effort to develop an artificial international language called "Esperanto" but it never really caught on.

However, English did.

English is the most widely spoken, read and understood language on earth when you consider both first and second languages because it's the most popular second language in the world. This is not surprising if you consider these points:

- *The British presence around the world for centuries.*
- *The U.S. presence in Europe and Asia following World War II.*
- *American culture, including movies, television shows and music, especially popular music among the young.*

As a result, much of your business communication can be conducted in English.

Be aware that for many people with whom you're communicating English is their second language:

1. *Avoid slang.*
2. *Use simpler (shorter) vocabulary words wherever possible.*

TRADING FROM BOTH ENDS

In considering the world of export and import, remember that each of those words refers to one end of a transaction. If you export a product, someone has to be importing it in another country. If you import a product, someone has to be exporting it from another country. So export and import are two sides of the same coin.

If you have started with a plan either to export product for sale overseas or to import goods for resale here think of that as your starting point, not your ending point. Many people start with one in mind and end up busily involved in both importing and exporting.

If you start by exporting, before long some of your buyers will send you their catalogs with information on products they have available for export to the United States. If you start by importing, before long your seller will write and ask if you can help locate a particular product that he would like to consider importing from the United States. So look at international trade from both points of view; specialize in one area to start off, but keep an open mind to the other end of things.

When I discuss shipping, documentation and payments, I will start from the exporter's point of view, as I have successfully done in all my seminars and classes. By understanding the steps of an export transaction, you know how to sell the goods, collect the money, and ship the goods overseas. When you switch to an import transaction, you simply reverse the procedure: Buy the goods, arrange to send the money, and bring the goods in from overseas. Then add customs procedures and you are on your way. For the time being, you will work your transactions in U.S. dollars to make it even easier. So if your main interest is import, please don't skip ahead.

You need to know how export works to really understand import.

GET IN ON IMPORTING

Here are three big reasons to consider importing:

1. *Because of what economists call comparative advantage, manufacturers in some foreign countries are able to make products more cheaply than domestic manufacturers.*
2. *Some products available overseas may not be available in the U.S. market . . . yet. Until you bring them in.*
3. *Sometimes the entire United States is available as an exclusive sales territory for an aggressive importer.*

Quality Is the Key

What U.S. products sell best overseas? On the largest scale, we all know their names: Burger King, Kentucky Fried Chicken, McDonald's and Pizza Hut. Then there are U.S.-made television programs, rock music and movies. What do these products have in common? In their respective fields, they are considered simply the best in the world.

Don't deal in junk. Nobody wants it. Deal in quality. Try to be the best in the world. That is what the world wants. As an importer, too—whether your product is paper clips, fine jewelry or solar technology—be sure that what you have is the best in the world.

Keep the perspective of your customer—the one who pays the bills and generates the profits—in mind at all times. But the most important thing of all, in getting started in world trade profitably, is to take action!

IT'S TIME TO GET STARTED

Have you ever noticed that once you learn a new word, no matter how many syllables or how difficult it was to learn, you begin seeing it and hearing it almost everywhere? Once you decide that you are going to enter the exciting and potentially profitable world of international trade, you begin to find resources almost everywhere.

The real challenge I have found with many of my students and clients is not one of information being too scarce but of information overload. It's tempting to keep searching, examining materials, going to seminars, and spending endless hours at the library, feeling that you never know quite enough to get started.

While there is plenty to know and there is always something more to learn, your success in international trade depends not just on how much you know but also on how much action you take with what you know. I challenge you to get started with your export or import business after reading just the next few chapters.

If you are interested in export, I challenge you that by the end of chapter two you should have written at least two or three letters to prospective buyers about products you want to export. At this stage they may be general, and you may not even have as much advertising material ready to send as you want. You can still get started.

Here is an incentive beyond profit. After three years of exporting, you can file an application with your local office of the U.S. Department of Commerce for the "E" Award for Export Expansion. This is awarded to you by the secretary of commerce on behalf of the president.

If you are interested in import, I challenge you that by the end of chapter three you should have written at least two or three letters to prospective sources for the types of products you want to import. You may not have as many specifics yet as you wish, but you can certainly get started.

Go through the next few chapters and learn where to get some addresses of prospective customers and suppliers and get started tomorrow! Remember, at this point you are supplying information or asking for information, so you are not obligating yourself or your company. To help you get started, I have drafted some generic letters to help you on either export or import or both (see pages 21 and 25). Use them as a model.

CHAPTER TWO

Finding Markets for Products Abroad

- *Libraries*

- *Finding Federal Assistance*

- *State and Local Assistance*

- *World Trade Centers*

- *Attending Classes and Seminars*

- *The Small Business Administration*

- *Journal of Commerce*

- *Know What Kind of Assistance You Need*

- *Writing to Your Prospects*

There are so many sources for locating prospects abroad that it is sometimes difficult to know where to begin.

Many of my new clients have been active in sales within the United States for many years, but they have received an inquiry from overseas and are unsure how to handle it. Some leads may have already walked into your office by themselves. Unsolicited leads might come in:

- Through your advertising in U.S. magazines, especially magazines specific to your trade.
- Through publicity items about your product in a trade magazine or other publication (always an excellent form of advertising).
- Through your participation in a trade show in the United States that attracted foreign buyers.
- Through your product itself. Your product may already be overseas because a visitor to the United States purchased it for personal use and took it home. Other people noticed the product, were impressed, and wrote to you.

Sometimes these leads are from individuals who would like to buy a quantity of one and have you send it to them by mail. Oftentimes, a potential international distributor is impressed enough to write and inquire about buying wholesale quantities for import into his country.

But there are many other sources of leads. Here are enough to keep you and your staff busy for some time to come.

STEPS IN AN EXPORT TRANSACTION

As you'll see in the upcoming chapters, these are the twelve steps to any successful export transaction:

1. *Contact prospects (mail, fax, trade shows) with export price list, catalogs, sales materials.*
2. *Follow up.*
3. *Obtain request for pro forma invoice.*
4. *Obtain clarification as needed (special documents).*
5. *Obtain quotations and requirements from freight forwarder.*
6. *Send pro forma invoice.*
7. *Receive letter of credit.*
8. *Contact banker and forwarder for advice.*
9. *Manufacture or purchase goods.*
10. *Ship goods.*
11. *Receive payment.*
12. *Continue to follow up with customers.*

LIBRARIES

Your local libraries, and the people who work in them, can be a gold mine of information. Ask a librarian for assistance. Sometimes all the material on world trade is in one reference section, sometimes not. Some material may be on microfilm or microfiche, and the librarian can show you exactly how to use these systems. Best of all, sometimes the materials can be checked out.

The Public Library

Most public libraries have reference materials on international trade. There are many technical books on statistics as well as operations-oriented books on documentation and logistics you can refer to later if needed. Right now, look for books such as *The International Directory of Importers*, through which you can locate importers for a specific type of product in a specific country.

You will probably also find many country-specific books (often published by foreign chambers of commerce), listing importers in their city, province or country and industry-specific books (published by, for example, photographic supply, industrial machinery or other trade groups) listing importers.

You will also find some directories of exporters from the United States. (Some are in the Resource List of this book.) It is worth your while to write to the publishers with information about your company and product, asking to be listed in future editions. Because the books are published annually or biannually, it can take some time for your listing to appear. But when it does appear, people overseas will track you down to find the U.S. products that you list as your exports.

Cost: Usually free.

University and College Libraries

Almost any institution of higher learning has a good reference section on world trade. Those that offer majors in the field, or at least a substantial number of courses, have a great deal available. Public institutions generally offer their reference services to the public; private institutions do so sometimes. Some state universities offer the taxpayers a library card for a nominal fee to check out circulating books just like the tuition-paying students!

Cost: Free, or nominal for a borrower's card.

FINDING FEDERAL ASSISTANCE

The U.S. Department of Commerce has many responsibilities—taking the census and handling patents and trademarks, to name just two. Assisting U.S. exporters also falls under the umbrella of this governmental department.

U.S. and Foreign Commercial Service

The specific office responsible for assisting exporters is the U.S. and Foreign Commer-

cial Service (US&FCS) with offices in most states. Make sure you visit their office. Their entire purpose for existing is to carry out the U.S. government policy of stimulating exports. There is such a policy for two principal reasons:

1. Stimulating exports of goods (and services as well) helps fight the trade deficit.
2. It generates new business, meaning new profits and new jobs. Profits increase tax collections. New jobs take people off the unemployment rolls and produce new tax revenues.

The US&FCS takes its responsibility very seriously and will do all it can to help you. Make this one of your first stops in your exporting plan.

Reference

Most of the offices have very good reference libraries of their own, covering a great many aspects of international trade. Many directories can be found there to help you find leads from overseas.

Cost: Free.

Consulting Services

The US&FCS has international trade specialists who will meet with you to help you develop export sales. Their programs are primarily oriented toward locating markets and identifying potential buyers in those markets.

Call for an appointment first, so you will have a definite period of time allotted to you. Bring your advertising materials, catalogs, and any leads you have already received.

Cost: I used to call this a free service, but sometimes I found my students did not take proper advantage of it. Then I realized some of them thought something that was "free" could not have much value. So let's describe the cost this way: When you paid your taxes April 15, you prepaid for this service. So you might as well make use of what you have already paid for.

Trade Opportunities Program

The Trade Opportunities Program (TOPS) is a computer database you can tie into from your home or office computer. It is a collection of trade leads that the US&FCS has collected from resources all over the world. (They have a representative in most U.S. consulates abroad.) The listings indicate the countries and the types of products wanted, followed by the contact persons, addresses, telephone and fax numbers, etc. It is updated daily, so you have current information to work from.

Cost: $35, plus a fee for the amount of time you spend on-line with the computer.

If you do not have a computer or modem, you can examine many leads in the *Journal of Commerce* (see page 20). Many leads are also available in the monthly updated National Trade Data Bank (see page 18).

ECONOMIC BULLETIN BOARD

Another program offered by the U.S. Department of Commerce is the Economic Bulletin Board.

For exporters and other businesses, it provides information similar to that of the National Trade Data Bank, but it is updated constantly. It includes daily leads from the Trade Opportunities Program (TOPS).

The cost is currently $45 per year, which includes two hours of connect time. Additional connect time ranges from five cents to forty cents per minute depending on time of day and baud rate of modem.

Full information is available from the U.S. Department of Commerce at (202) 482-1986.

Export Contact List Service

This service provides you with names and addresses of companies interested in your particular product or service, available in printed form or on mailing labels. They come from many sources and can be ordered by country, by continent or worldwide, at twenty-five cents each.

This is an excellent source of information for mass mailings of catalogs, price lists or other advertising information used to solicit agents or distributors.

Agent/Distributor Service

In this program, you supply the US&FCS office with catalogs and other information you have available on your products or services. They will send the material to their office in the country of your choice. The Department of Commerce representatives there will circulate your materials and attempt to find prospects who express an interest after seeing the material. The leads are then supplied to you, down to the specific individual to contact. This gives your mailing the personal touch in the importer's country and also supplies you with up-to-date information.

Cost: $250 per country

Publications

The U.S. and Foreign Commercial Service (US&FCS) can introduce you to many publications that you can purchase or subscribe to in order to build your own international reference library. Most are inexpensive; some are available at no cost.

I highly recommend "A Basic Guide to Exporting," an inexpensive guide to export from start to finish. If you are interested in trading with Eastern Europe, subscribe to the free Eastern Europe Business Bulletin (see Resource List).

Country and Industry Specialists

In addition to the assistance available at the local office, specialists in Washington, DC, are available to answer questions on specific situations by phone.

There is a desk officer for most countries in the world, as well as ones for the European Community and other groups of countries. There are also other specialists available who cover major industries on a worldwide basis.

You can obtain an up-to-date list of direct numbers when you visit the US&FCS office. The central number, from which you can be connected to any desk officer, is (202) 482-2000.

FINDING NICHE MARKETS ABROAD

You may not be able to successfully compete with the largest U.S. exporters, but there are niches to fill in any industry.

Among our biggest exports is medical technology. While you may not be able to get into the business of exporting the latest and most expensive high-tech equipment, that leaves niches that larger companies are not always interested in filling.

In some countries around the world, the largest and most advanced hospitals still have never seen a disposable hypodermic needle (and are reusing needles after sterilizing them in between patients).

In the photographic industry, a few U.S. companies make colored paper backgrounds for photographers and export by ocean around the world.

In the automotive industry, there are dozens of items (logo key chains, fire extinguishers and first aid kits to carry in the trunk, beverage cup holders, trunk organizer systems, visor pockets) that the large companies don't get involved with.

Trade Shows

The US&FCS sponsors trade shows, sometimes at our own trade centers (in Mexico City, for example), where several U.S. companies in a particular industry promote their individual products to prospective buyers while promoting the American industry as well. The US&FCS promotes the show and brings in importers. At some very large trade shows, the US&FCS leases a large amount of floor space and sublets it to individual U.S. companies. Often, they arrange to consolidate shipments of exhibit materials.

This can be an expensive option, but it's less expensive than working on your own.

Catalog and Videotape Shows

For catalog shows, you can send your catalogs and literature for distribution to visitors at the U.S. booth without going to the expense of sending a representative of your own. There are also shows set up with videotapes, making presentations for the U.S. products.

With either of these alternatives the impact is less, of course, than if you had a sales representative present, but the cost is very low, sometimes just a few hundred dollars for a major industry show.

Foreign Buyers and Matchmaker Programs

The Foreign Buyers Program exhibits materials in the United States and brings foreign buyers to the exhibit. The Matchmaker Program takes U.S. exporters to specific countries, or groups of countries, to keep pre-set appointments with foreign importers. Office space is provided for meetings with prospective buyers.

USA TRADE

The U.S. Department of Commerce maintains a central number as a clearinghouse for information. Call (800) USA TRADE (872-8723).

The staff can provide information on getting started in exporting and can also supply information helpful to the new exporter.

USA XPORT

This is a fax retrieval system providing information on the potential for exporting to more than seventy countries, including information on specific industries. Many specific trade leads are also listed.

Call (800) USA XPORT (872-9767) *from a fax machine.* The computer will walk you through the steps to get a registration form. Once you complete and return it, you can download information.

Cost: There is no charge to sign up for the program and get started.

The National Trade Data Bank

The National Trade Data Bank is produced by the Economics and Statistics Administration of the Department of Commerce. This is a CD-ROM that can access more than 90,000 documents. Its information includes statistics on industries and countries that can show you which countries are the major importers for your type of product.

The information is updated monthly. Your local Department of Commerce office can advise you if any public or college libraries in your area also have it available.

Cost: Free at libraries; $360 per year for subscription.

STATE AND LOCAL ASSISTANCE

As part of the U.S. Department of Commerce's mission to stimulate exports, every state has a department, or a section within a department, with the same assignment. Many larger cities do, also.

These departments go by different names in different areas. Their concentration in the area of export is similar to the federal government's goals—to stimulate exports in order to stimulate jobs, as well as profits, in their jurisdictions.

Services available include many of the services available at the federal level: joint trade fairs, consulting services, trade missions, etc.

Many state and local departments of commerce publish their own directory of exporters, and will give you a listing with information about your company and products. The books are then distributed worldwide through mailings and trade shows at no cost to you. They are often sent to a list of public libraries overseas.

These directories come out once a year or once every two years, so it may be a while before you benefit from it. But once you are listed, you are in a book that circulates for quite a while.

International offices are also opening in many major cities, such as Tokyo, Taipei, Paris and Mexico City, to help domestic companies promote their products for export. Some of these offices contain permanent showrooms. Others have meeting rooms and attempt to set up appointments for you with prospective buyers on your visit to that city.

Bring some of your advertising literature with you on your visit to your state or city office and ask that it be sent to the foreign offices. The people in the foreign offices will work to get you leads to follow up.

Cost: Many services are free. Trade fairs and foreign missions vary in cost.

AGRICULTURAL EXPORTS

Food and agricultural products are among the United States's biggest exports. The best place to start for foreign market information is the U.S. Department of Agriculture's Trade Assistance and Promotion Office which can be reached by telephone at (202) 720-7420 or fax at (202) 690-4374.

Another excellent resource is the AgExport Connection of the Department of Agriculture, which will send you a free AgExport Action Kit to help get you started. Call (202) 720-7103 or fax (202) 690-4374.

WORLD TRADE CENTERS

The World Trade Centers operate on an international basis, offering many services to the prospective exporter or importer.

The primary service of immediate value to the individual business person is a bulletin board system on which you can post your own leads and download leads of others. Thus, you can advertise your products and indicate the products you may be looking for. You can also download the postings that other businesses around the world have placed.

Most World Trade Centers, all affiliated on a worldwide basis, have local networking functions for members, informative programs, publications and other services.

Fee: An annual membership fee, which varies.

If you have difficulty finding a World Trade Center locally, contact the World Trade Centers Association Headquarters at One World Trade Center, Suite 7701, New York, NY 10048 (212) 313-4600.

ATTENDING CLASSES AND SEMINARS

You do not have to study for a degree to take advantage of college courses. Many universities and colleges offer individual courses and seminars in international business that you can attend as a nondegree ("nonmatriculated") student.

Non-college-credit seminars are available in many subjects, including international trade. These will be for a morning or an afternoon, all day or several days. Check into the short-term seminars to start off.

Many classes are available in the evenings. A one-credit course may meet three hours, one evening a week, for five weeks. A three-credit course usually meets the whole semester.

When you check into the courses and seminars, be sure you examine the course descriptions carefully. Some courses are designed to help the business person interested in getting into international trade beginning at a small level, while others are for graduate students in economics who are studying the international balance of payments and national policies toward trade deficits. Just be sure you sign up for one that is right for you.

I emphasize contacting your local community colleges because they are usually heavily subsidized by taxing authority and have extremely low tuition. Many have excellent international courses in the evenings, taught by people who are active in the field during the day and also attend seminars.

Cost: Varies.

THE SMALL BUSINESS ADMINISTRATION

I do not want to overemphasize the Small Business Administration (SBA) as a source of funds or loan guarantees because there is heavy competition for the funds that are available, and there are never enough to go around. They do have loans available, including loans specifically for international trade, and other loans and loan guarantee programs (including those for working capital) for which you may qualify. Just remember that you will be vying with many other small business owners. As a source of free assistance, however, the Small Business Administration can be indispensable.

Consulting Services

Ask about the SBA's consulting programs, including SCORE (Service Corps of Retired Executives). These people have spent a lifetime learning their field and, now retired, are eager to share the information with people still actively building their businesses.

They will meet with you by appointment to share their expertise and help your company grow. The expertise available is not limited to international trade, by the way. They have experts in purchasing, marketing, advertising and other areas as well.

Cost: Free.

ATLAS

ATLAS is a free service of the SBA that provides data reports on countries and products. It stands for Automated Trade Locator Assistance System and can give you important statistical information on your potential exports. Contact your local SBA office.

Small Business Development Centers

Most often Small Business Development Centers (SBDCs) are run through community colleges but with funding from the SBA. They have consultants currently active in the field, who will meet with you at no charge (or, if you prefer, you prepaid for their services on April 15). Some are owners of their own businesses; some are managers of a business.

As with SCORE, their consultants come with expertise in many different areas. International trade is usually a priority.

SBDCs usually have small but very good reference libraries on business subjects.

Cost: Free.

JOURNAL OF COMMERCE

A good resource with a great deal of international news is the *Journal of Commerce*, 445 Marshall Street, Phillipsburg, NJ 08865-9984. It's a daily newspaper with one full page dedicated to export leads every day.

Articles cover many aspects of international trade. A listing of international trade shows is a regular feature.

Cost: As one of our readers, a free one-week trial subscription is available to you by calling (800) 221-3777; a one-year subscription is $325.

DON'T EXPECT IT TO BE "EASY MONEY"

Those who get involved in international trade expecting to make an easy (and quick) dollar usually end up losing money.

First, you should be in it for the long haul, not to sell any customer once, but to sell many customers repeatedly over the years. That's where the real profits are.

Second, if the product doesn't sell in the domestic market, don't expect to make millions selling it to foreign importers. Many products are available at discounted, liquidated prices because nobody wants them.

KNOW WHAT KIND OF ASSISTANCE YOU NEED

With so much assistance available to you at little or no cost, you can easily see that you have the expertise and the framework available for your export plans to come to fruition. Later on, we will meet the foreign freight forwarder and international banker, who will also be ready to work with you as your plans begin to gel.

I urge this: When you go for assistance, other than taking courses or seminars, know what you want. You should have a specific product, or preferably a group of products, to talk about. It does not hurt to have a specifically targeted country or group of countries either, but you may need some direction in narrowing down your possibilities.

Some people have said that they have gone to my resources, and the resources have been of little or no help. The real problem is that the client did not know what he or she wanted.

I put it to you this way: What if someone went to your local public library to find and check out a book, and the conversation with the librarian went something like this:

READER: *Hello, I'd like to check out a book, please.*
LIBRARIAN: Of course. On what subject?
READER: *I dunno.*
LIBRARIAN: Is there a particular subject you're most interested in?
READER: *I dunno.*
LIBRARIAN: Well, is there a certain author you particularly enjoy?
READER: *No, not really.*
LIBRARIAN: Fiction or nonfiction, for heaven's sake?

Well, you get the idea. Have a clear idea of what you are looking for before you start out, and you will have the right questions to ask. If you do this correctly, you will be getting requests for quotations in no time (chapters five and six discuss quotations at length).

WRITING TO YOUR PROSPECTS

Here is a more or less generic letter that you can adapt to send out with your existing advertising literature. Consider raising your prices just a little to give you room to negotiate when you begin to get replies. People in other countries sometimes see a sales price as a starting point for negotiation.

Dear:

We recently obtained your name and address as a leading importer of recreational fishing equipment. At the present time, we are very interested in obtaining a distributor in Japan for our products.

We enclose herewith our full catalog, as well as our current price list, and believe you will find both the products and the pricing extremely competitive.

These products are selling very successfully in the United States, and we believe they would enjoy strong popularity in your market as well.

Our terms of sale are ex works, Omaha, Nebraska, U.S.A., payable by sight letter of credit in U.S. dollars on a U.S. bank.

Should you be more interested in other products, we would appreciate receiving your specifications as we can often supply items not in our present catalog.

We thank you for your time in examining our material, and we look forward to hearing from you.

Very truly yours,

Finding Sources for Products Abroad

- *U.S. Customs and the Importer*
- *Hooking Into the Importer's Network*
- *Writing to Your Suppliers*
- *Avoiding the Pitfalls*

Many of the resources available to help you in exporting products from the United States are also available to help you when you are interested in importing. Small Business Development Centers, and especially the library, will help.

I particularly emphasize the library because in the international reference section you should find several directories of exporters from various countries. Send them a letter or a fax and ask for their catalog, export prices and other information.

If you skipped the last chapter because you are interested in importing rather than exporting, go back and read about those export resources now and use them for import.

Resources of lesser assistance to importers are the U.S. Department of Commerce and its state and city counterparts. They do an excellent job, but their assignment is specifically to stimulate exports, not imports. You may find, however, that reference materials available through them will help you.

The following are sources that offer assistance specifically to importers.

U.S. CUSTOMS AND THE IMPORTER

Congress has assigned the U.S. Customs Service two missions:

1. To protect and collect the revenue due the United States. Primarily, this is duty (tariffs). But Customs collects some IRS excise taxes, too, primarily on liquor.
2. To protect the laws of the United States, the individual states and the jurisdictions within. The Customs Service watches for goods that someone is trying to bring into the United

States in violation of the law, ranging from illegal drugs to merchandise infringing on a patent, copyright or trademark.

You will find more about what Customs does in chapters eleven and twelve. But one of the things Customs does not do is assist you in finding sources for products from overseas. This is not part of their responsibilities. Customs does not have time for it, and since they do know what importers are bringing in, they are specifically forbidden by law to discuss one importer's business with another, or with anyone else. So to remain in compliance with the law, Customs cannot give you a source. They would generally only know about a source for the product you want if someone else is already bringing it in.

This is very different from the U.S. and Foreign Commercial Service. They have a completely different role in the government. But I do encourage you to visit the U.S. Customs Service office in your city. First, if you are going to be importing, you should know where Customs is. Second, Customs usually has a variety of pamphlets to give away on various subjects of interest to you, including quotas, tariff classifications and other areas.

Ask, too, for a free list of Customs Brokers currently holding permits to do business in your area. (We will meet Customs Brokers in chapter four.)

Any time you plan a trip to a foreign country, stop by the Customs Service office for two things: (1) Pick up a copy of "Know Before You Go," which contains information on duties, prohibited merchandise, and other legal and regulatory issues for the person returning to the United States from a trip. (2) If you are taking a foreign-made camera, jewelry or other expensive items on your trip, especially if they are new, register them with Customs in your city first. This service is quick and free. You will get paperwork to present as you go through customs when you return. It proves you did not buy the expensive merchandise overseas, so you will not be forced to pay duty on it.

HOOKING INTO THE IMPORTER'S NETWORK

Finding good suppliers isn't always easy, but a variety of services and organizations can be of tremendous help in locating products you want to import.

Foreign Consulates

As we discussed in chapter two, the U.S. and Foreign Commercial Service of the U.S. Department of Commerce has offices in U.S. consulates overseas whose assignment is to help stimulate U.S. exports. Likewise, foreign governments have offices in their consulates here in the United States whose mission is to stimulate their countries' exports to us (our imports from them).

A large or even medium-sized city may have several consulates, particularly from the larger countries of the world. Their services vary but are generally along the lines of the services rendered by the U.S. and Foreign Commercial Service.

To locate consulates in your city (or the nearest large city), try:

- White Pages under "Consulate of _____"
- Yellow Pages under "Consulates"
- State or city department of commerce (government)
- State or city chamber of commerce (private)
- World Trade Center
- Libraries

Cost: Usually free unless it involves a trip to their country. (You are the importer, so you are the customer this time.)

WHERE TO LOOK

Check these resources for the products you want to import.

- *Foreign consulates (obtain locations from your public library)*
- *Directories of importers (public library)*
- *Trade organizations*
- *Trade journals*
- *Trade shows*
- *Trade leads published in business publications*

Importers' Directories

Importers' directories are published annually or biannually, but if you get your company and your needs listed in the next issues of major international directories, the foreign companies that sell those products will find you. A few such directories are listed in the Resource List in the back of this book, but when you visit your library, take down the addresses of others you find. Write to all of them. You never know exactly which listing will get you the precise information you want.

Trade Associations

If you are planning to import a particular type of product, naturally it is one you are familiar with. So you may already belong to the trade association for that product, be it textbooks, paper clips or solar technology. Many trade associations have members on an international basis, and their directories include members around the world, listed by types of products they handle or manufacture. If your particular trade association is on a U.S.-only membership basis, they can put you in touch with an international association or supply you with names and addresses of related associations in foreign countries.

Foreign Chambers of Commerce

Most chambers of commerce around the world are eager to circulate trade leads among their memberships. Send a letter to a chamber of commerce outlining your needs and ask them to publish the information in their newsletter. This should get responses.

The addresses of chambers of commerce can be obtained from the local library, but I have also seen letters sent with the city address, (Chamber of Commerce, Tokyo, Japan), and the local post office knew where they were.

STEPS IN AN IMPORT TRANSACTION

By the end of the book, you'll know all ten steps to a successful import transaction.

1. *Obtain price lists, catalogs, sales materials.*
2. *Obtain samples.*
3. *Contact a Customs Broker.*
4. *Contact any other government agencies as appropriate.*
5. *Request pro forma invoice, advising the exporter of documentation needs, time frames, etc.*
6. *Be certain of all costs, time frames needed and regulations.*
7. *Obtain as many buying commitments as possible before importing.*
8. *Advise the Customs Broker when goods are expected and carrier to be used.*
9. *Fill orders promptly.*
10. *Follow up with all customers.*

Government Trade Associations

Many government-linked trade associations are primarily geared toward promoting exports from a particular country, although some also distribute information on U.S. products for potential importers back home. One of the largest such associations is the Japan External Trade Organization

(JETRO). Another excellent organization is the Hong Kong Trade Development Council. Ask for a copy of the Hong Kong Enterprise, a periodic catalog of goods available for sale to the United States. (See the Resource List for addresses and phone numbers for JETRO and the Hong Kong Trade Development Council.)

WRITING TO YOUR SUPPLIERS

In writing to prospective suppliers, request their catalog and other sales materials and their best export prices. You can follow the sample letter below, customizing it as needed. The phrase "best export prices" is commonly used right from the beginning, although you will ordinarily receive a standard price list or schedule of discounts. Sometimes there is still room to negotiate.

Keep in mind that some of the information you receive from prospective suppliers will be in metric measures (weights and dimensions), so some conversion will probably be necessary. Also, in many countries, items are packed in multiples of ten rather than twelve.

Dear:

We recently obtained your name and address as a leading supplier of recreational fishing equipment. At the present time, we are very interested in importing fishing equipment from Japan to add to our catalog.

We request that you send us your current catalog and best export prices, and any samples that would assist us in evaluating your products.

We thank you for your time in sending us the material, and we look forward to examining it and preparing an opening order.

Very truly yours,

SAMPLES

Samples are extremely important for consumer products, regardless of how many specifications are sent back and forth.

As a U.S. importer, be sure the labeling meets U.S. requirements, so you won't have to relabel each box or jar after arrival.

As a U.S. exporter, ensure that the shipment is not delayed or complicated by something your importer did not anticipate.

Most sellers will furnish a few samples gratis to serious buyers except for expensive merchandise for which a charge is sometimes made, equal to approximately the wholesale cost. Shipping is usually borne by the seller.

With a sample that might be sent airfreight, the seller may agree to furnish it at no charge if the buyer is willing to pay the freight on a freight collect basis.

AVOIDING THE PITFALLS

We will get into details about U.S. requirements for imported products in chapters eleven and twelve. For now, bear in mind that products manufactured in foreign countries are generally made for their own market, unless the company you are buying from is exclusively manufacturing for export. So watch for differences and for additional expenses you may have.

- If the item is an electrical product, will it work on our electrical systems, or will it come in ready for hookup to a 220-volt system? Or will it have incompatible prongs?
- Will instructions be in English or will you have to have the instructions translated and reprinted yourself? Will the packaging be in English or will new packaging have to be printed?
- Will the manufacturer be able to supply spare parts for repairs? Will you receive credit on future orders for warranty service you had to provide?
- Will the product meet requirements in the United States for Underwriters Laboratory, or other certifying groups, as well as U.S. and local government laws and regulations?

It is very important that you obtain a sample of the merchandise before actually importing, to satisfy yourself as to the quality of the product and to submit it for whatever testing may be appropriate.

Many firms charge retail price plus postage for a sample. This protects them against people who only want to write away for free samples of whatever they can get their hands on, who may have no intention of importing commercially. Some credit this payment against your first order. Other firms supply samples at no charge.

The Formula for Success

A major difference between exporting and importing is that exporting is much simpler than importing. Import requires the same financial and shipping transactions as does export, but there is more to it.

On an export shipment, once you export the products and have ensured that you are getting paid, you're done. On an import shipment, after the goods arrive and you have sent your money, you still have to clear the goods through Customs and then find buyers for the goods in order to make your profit.

So, as you accumulate information on potential imports, here is my "Magic Formula for Successful Importing":

1. Know that you can sell the product at a profit. Before figuring your profits, know all your costs and build in an extra margin for Murphy's Law (the unexpected delay or expense).
2. Know that you can conform to all applicable laws and regulations

without exception, so there will be no fines or penalties, nor will goods be seized by the Customs Service or other authorities.

3. Have enough definite buyers for your goods at least to break even promptly after shipment, before you go to additional buyers.

If you follow these three steps, you will be off to a strong start!

CHAPTER FOUR

Where to Go for Help

- *The International Bank*
- *The International Freight Forwarder*
- *The Customs Broker*
- *The Composite Office*

Here, I will discuss some of the cast of characters—the specialists in international trade to whom you can go, should go, and, for your own success, *must* go for help. Just as in your domestic business you do not have to know how the banking system works to deposit a check, you do not have to know how a trucking company is run in order to ship. You simply have to know what services you need, whom to contact for those services, and how best to utilize them for your business.

THE INTERNATIONAL BANK

You don't have to go to New York, Chicago, Houston or Los Angeles to do your international banking. Any city with a population of more than 500,000 probably has an international bank. The bank may not have a strange or exotic name; in fact, it may be the bank you do business with already. You can arrange letters of credit, sight drafts (more about these in chapter seven), international money orders, wire transfers, and just about anything else you will need locally.

Call the main office of your bank, or any of the larger banks in your area, to see if they have an international department. If they don't, ask if they know of a nearby bank that does.

You do not have to switch over all your regular banking business to the bank you select as your international banker. If you do deal with your own bank, the international department will be delighted to have your new additional business. If you use a different bank, the only difference is that you will have to run some documents between the banks.

If you receive $10,000 under a letter of credit and it is your own bank, the international department can simply, following your standing instructions, deposit the money into your account and call to notify you that the funds are available for you to draw upon immediately (then they will send you a written confirmation). If it is a different bank, the only difference is you will have to ask them to mail you their cashier's check for the $10,000 or have it available at their counter for you or a messenger to pick up.

I suggest that you visit an international banker early on. (But read at least through chapter seven first.) Explain what you are planning to export or import, and ask them to explain the international services they have available and what their fees are. They should be able to give you a printed list of charges for everything from letters of credit to international money orders.

ABOUT EXPERTISE AND EXPERTS

In starting your own business, it's helpful to have a knowledge of accounting and business law. But that doesn't mean you have to go to law school and also become a CPA to start a business. You should have a basic understanding, and rely on your attorney and accountant when needed.

Likewise, you don't have to become an expert on import and export. You need a basic understanding of the terminology and the procedures involved. Then you need reliable experts to depend on.

The key experts are:
- *International bankers*
- *Freight Forwarders*
- *Customs Brokers*

Banking Correspondents

If you plan to work with business people in a specific foreign country, ask your international banker if the bank has a branch in that country. If your bank is not very large, it probably has *correspondents*—banks in that country with whom it has a steady, ongoing relationship to take care of each other's customers' business. Many times, an international banker has checking accounts in the correspondent's bank (in lire, pounds, francs, marks, or whatever the local currency is, as well as one in dollars), and the correspondent has accounts with the U.S. bank.

Learning this information about your international banker is not just to satisfy your curiosity. You and the business people with whom you work overseas need to transfer monies as efficiently as possible. If you can tell your foreign associates who your bank's correspondent is in Milan, London, Paris or Frankfurt, it can make your business relationship much easier.

THE INTERNATIONAL FREIGHT FORWARDER

An international freight forwarder is like a travel agent who deals with freight rather than passengers and is only involved in international dealings.

The international freight forwarder is your specialist when it comes to shipping the goods. There are two types of international freight forwarders—the Federal Maritime Commission Forwarder and the Air Freight Forwarder.

SPECIALISTS AT THE U.S. DEPARTMENT OF COMMERCE

The U.S. Department of Commerce has expert help available for exporters.

Country desk officers can provide expert help on exporting to specific countries.

Commodity specialists can be contacted for expert help on specific commodities.

These personnel are located in Washington, DC. Contact your local U.S. Department of Commerce office for direct phone numbers.

The Federal Maritime Commission Forwarder

The Federal Maritime Commission (FMC) forwarder specializes in handling ocean shipments. These forwarders are regulated and licensed by the Federal Maritime Commission under the Shipping Acts of 1916 and 1984, and they post a performance bond to stay licensed.

Each FMC forwarder is licensed to advertise to the general public to act as a forwarder of freight (often called *cargo* in ocean shipping) for clients to its ultimate destination.

I will discuss ocean shipping first because I would hope most of your export shipments will be large enough to be ocean shipments.

Among the services rendered by an FMC forwarder are:

- Quoting ocean freight rates
- Quoting of truck, rail or other freight rates for services needed to move the shipment to port
- Making arrangements for the above, to ensure speedy and safe movement of the goods
- Preparing documents needed for international shipping
- Ensuring the above conform to special requirements, such as a letter of credit

Once you have a shipment, the freight forwarder ensures that it is efficiently moved to its destination and that all documents are in order.

Choosing a Forwarder

So you call a freight forwarder once you have a shipment, right? Wrong!

In the first place, you call a freight forwarder when you are first quoting an order so you know your costs in advance. By the same token, you need to know the document requirements for a particular destination and the time frames involved. Otherwise, what happens if you have an order with two weeks to ship and it takes three weeks to get the shipment ready?

In the second place, the best time to get to know a forwarder is before you need his services. You can generally find forwarders in the Yellow Pages under "Freight Forwarders," and the FMC forwarders usually list those letters or their license number in an ad. You can also get a list of forwarders from the U.S. Department of Commerce or your state's department of commerce.

Contact a freight forwarder (or two, or three, to see which one you feel most comfortable with), and make an appointment to talk about your plans. You need not get into specifics. You can discuss a general type of commodity to a particular country or part of the world. Ask about documentation requirements, the company's background, and the experience of the people in the office. Some FMC forwarders are part of international forwarding firms with dozens of offices around the country and literally hundreds of offices around the globe. There are also independent firms with one office and a small staff, and there are medium-sized companies in between. Go on down to the office, learn who is who and what is what, and decide in whom you have confidence. Ask for a printed price sheet of fees for their services.

Respecting the Forwarder's Time

Forwarders are often victims of people who want to pick someone's brain without paying for the information. Case in point: When I was with an FMC forwarder some years ago, we received dozens of telephone calls requesting rate information to Italy. Not only was it always the same commodity, but always the exact same size shipment: weight, number of crates, dimen-

sions of each crate and total value.

We backtracked and found out that a professor in international business at a local university had given his students the assignment of finding the cost of getting this exact shipment to Milan. Rather than do their homework, they all started calling forwarders to get their homework done for them!

A forwarder's job is really to move shipments, not to spend all day giving out free quotes. If you ask for their printed price schedule, or general information on documentation and how frequent sailings are to a particular port, they will be glad to talk with you. Then when you are giving a specific quotation to an overseas prospect, call back for a specific quote on a specific order.

The troublemaker, who ruins it for everyone, is the person who comes in and says: "I've been corresponding with people in twelve different countries and I'm preparing to go to a trade show where I may meet some of them. Would you please prepare a rate quote for me for each of the twelve countries? I'll need one for a 1,000-pound shipment, one for 2,000 pounds, one for 5,000 pounds, to each country, etc., etc." No one likes a freeloader. So stick to generalities until you have specific customers asking for specific quotes you really need.

The Air Freight Forwarder

An Air Freight Forwarder is simply a freight forwarder who specializes in air freight shipments. Other than being air-oriented instead of ocean, these forwarders render services similar to the services of ocean freight forwarders:

- Quoting air freight rates
- Quoting truck or other charges necessary to move the shipment to the airport, ready for shipment
- Making arrangements for the above, to

ensure speedy and safe movement of the goods

- Preparing documents needed for international shipping
- Ensuring the above conform to special requirements, such as a letter of credit

With air deregulation, there isn't much to stop anyone from hanging up a shingle as an air freight forwarder.

The International Air Transport Association (IATA) operated by the airlines having international service, does regulate who can act as an IATA agent, acting directly as an agent for the airlines. But plenty of people who are not IATA-affiliated are operating as air freight forwarders. This is perfectly legal, and most are 100 percent legitimate.

Just as there are large and small ocean freight forwarders, there are large and small air freight forwarders. Some companies have offices all over the world or all over the country. Many operate their own planes in addition to booking space on IATA aircraft. There are small, independent air freight forwarders; many are affiliated with very large companies, working as the company's local agents.

I suggest you look for the initials "IATA" in a yellow pages ad, although not all companies include them in their advertising. Such a designation may or may not be listed on a Department of Commerce list.

Again, it's best to schedule an informational interview with the forwarder. Examine the facility. Ask lots of questions:

- Are they affiliated with IATA?
- Are they affiliated with a national or international firm?
- Do they run some aircraft of their own?

The most valuable judgment is based on how comfortable you feel with the company and the people you meet.

Surface Shipments

You may need truck or rail shipments internationally, perhaps to Canada or to Mexico. In this area, there is no true freight forwarder as such.

Many trucking companies offer service to Canadian points, either through a Canadian subsidiary or with a Canadian trucking company working with them. For shipments to Mexico, it is often most efficient to arrange truck delivery to Brownsville, Laredo, Nogales or another border point, where the Mexican importer can arrange with a Customs Broker and a Mexican trucker to move the shipment to its final destination.

U.S. railroads can effectively make connections with both Canadian and Mexican railroads (Interline Service). However, both of these instances can involve insurance, documentation, and other requirements to be followed. Any ocean freight forwarder should be able to handle these requirements, as well as coordinate the entire shipment.

THE CUSTOMS BROKER

If you will be importing, the person you will work with on a regular basis is the Customs Broker. A Customs Broker is licensed by the Customs Service of the United States Treasury Department to assist importers with transactions.

Let me note a distinction between Customs Brokers and people who advertise their services as import brokers. An import broker is a person who has gotten into the business of buying and selling a certain commodity or commodities and has chosen that title for himself. He buys textiles and imports them for resale. This is not the same as a Customs Broker, and only a licensed Customs Broker can call himself that.

A Customs Broker is individually licensed by the government under very strict standards. The requirements are:

- He or she must be a U.S. citizen.
- He or she must be over eighteen.
- He or she must pass an extremely difficult written examination on both the *Customs Regulations of the United States* and the application of the *Harmonized Tariff Schedule of the United States* (the book that lists the customs duty to be paid for all import commodities from all countries).
- Before licensing, he or she must pass a thorough character investigation by U.S. Customs agents.

The Customs Service is very strict about who becomes a Customs Broker. This is partly because of the responsibility to the importer to ensure that all procedures are followed completely and lawfully. It is also because of a Custom Broker's responsibility to the government to ensure that the duty monies collected, sometimes hundreds of thousands of dollars, are turned over to the government when due.

A Customs Broker has a responsibility to both the importer and the government that the correct amount of duty is deposited with the Customs Service. Not too much (cheating the importer) and not too little (cheating the government), but exactly correct. Accuracy is key.

The responsibilities of a Customs Broker to both the importer and to the government involve knowledge, honesty, and a strict, meticulous attitude to paperwork. Many people who apply to become Customs Brokers never obtain the license.

Some brokerage firms are small offices where you may work directly with the Customs Broker. Others have dozens of offices around the country. But bear this in mind: To operate as a Customs Broker in your city, the firm must have a licensed Customs Broker on the premises, no matter how many Customs Brokers it has elsewhere. This is mandated by law: A licensed Customs Broker must be there to exercise supervision over the activities of the business.

SELLING TO THE NEWLY INDEPENDENT STATES

The U.S. Department of Commerce has an office specifically set up for exporters interested in selling to Russia and other states of the former Soviet Union: BISNIS (Business Information Service for the Newly Independent States). They can provide up-to-date information (often difficult to obtain elsewhere) on market data and regulations, and sources for trade leads.

The BISNIS Bulletin is a periodical available free upon request to potential exporters. BISNIS is located at the U.S. Department of Commerce, International Trade Administration, BISNIS, Room 7413, Washington, DC 20230, (202) 482-4655, fax: (202) 482-3145.

THE COMPOSITE OFFICE

Many companies offer one-stop service, providing an ocean (FMC) freight forwarder, an air freight forwarder and a Customs Broker. Such a company should be able to offer you most of the services you will need. Also, a composite office has two federal licenses and is subject to audit by both the Federal Maritime Commission and the U.S. Customs Service. Such a firm has high standards to meet.

EXPERT HELP FROM YOUR STATE DEPARTMENT OF COMMERCE

Your state department of commerce, usually located in your state's capital, is an important resource to the exporter.

The trade missions they sponsor are limited to people from your state.

They can offer you referrals to local forwarders, bankers and others.

They are familiar with the industry and economic conditions in your state.

Many have offices in foreign countries to seek out markets for your state's products.

Many have offices in several of a state's larger cities.

And, many U.S. cities now have their own offices to help exporters. Call your mayor's office to inquire.

CHAPTER FIVE

Terms of Sale

- *Damaged or Lost: Who Is Responsible?*

- *Pricing Variables*

In pricing exports or obtaining prices on imports, the question is not only "How much?" but also "Where?" The price you charge for a product when you are only responsible for delivering it to the pier is less than what you charge if you are responsible for moving the shipment all the way to Yokohama.

Another question under "How much?" is how much of the product is being bought or sold. You naturally charge a lower price for a person placing a $10,000 order than for a person placing a $1,000 order. That's business!

So pricing your product is a matter of:
- What the product is
- How much (or how many)
- How far the product is being moved at your expense

DAMAGED OR LOST: WHO IS RESPONSIBLE?

If goods are on board a ship and they arrive wet, who takes the loss? If goods are shipped from your location in good order but arrive at the port damaged, whose loss is it? Let's look at a domestic example.

Possession and Responsibility

Large's Department Store has a washing machine on sale for $300, and the price includes delivery to your door. You buy the washing machine and arrange for delivery. On the way, the truck is involved in a traffic accident, and the washing machine is damaged beyond repair.

Whose washing machine was it, yours or Large's? It is Large's machine because the price included delivery, and the machine had not been delivered (turned over) to you. Notice that we can all agree on this point regardless of how payment was arranged:

1. Cash at time of purchase, earlier in the week.

2. Large's nonrevolving credit plan (payment in full in thirty days).
3. Major credit card (payment to the bank issuing the credit card, immediately or in monthly payments).

In other words, terms of *payment* have nothing to do with the terms of *sale*.

Let's look at it from another angle. Large's Department Store sells the washing machine at $300. Delivery is $25 extra.

You can decide to arrange for the store to deliver the machine at an extra cost of $25—this is up to you. If Large's truck has an accident on the way and the machine is damaged, it is still Large's washing machine. They are responsible for sending you a new one at their expense. They cannot tell you that it was *your* machine that was damaged (if they try to, you will win in small claims court) because they had not yet turned it over to you.

Suppose you wanted to save the $25 and pick up the machine yourself. You borrow your brother-in-law's pickup truck and your brother-in-law, and off you go to pick up the machine. You and he have an accident on the way home, and the washing machine is damaged beyond repair. Whose washing machine was it? That's right, it was yours, and you don't have a case in small claims court. (You do if someone hit you, and you can prove it was their fault. But Large's is out of the picture. It was *your* machine that was damaged.)

The same holds true when the delivered price was $300 if you decided that you couldn't wait until next Saturday's free delivery run and arranged for you and your brother-in-law to pick it up. Once you had the washing machine in your possession— once it was properly turned over to you— it was yours, and you were responsible for it from there on.

Let's take another look at the situation.

Suppose you wanted to have the machine today but did not have your own truck available. So you called Speedee Delivery Service and arranged for them to make the pickup for you. If they have an accident on the way and the machine is damaged, yes, Speedee's is ultimately responsible and you can file a claim, but it was again your machine that was damaged.

Now let's get back to Large's. You made arrangements for them to make delivery but their delivery truck broke down. Their backup system is to hire Speedee Delivery Service. Now Speedee has the accident. It is up to Large's to file the claim with Speedee and also to send you out a new machine. It was still *their* machine that was damaged. This would be the case whether the $300 price included delivery or if delivery was an extra $25, which you agreed to pay, and regardless of when or how payment was made.

PRICING VARIABLES

Now let's switch to another business: the export book business.

You run a combination publishing company-distribution company-retail store, and you sell books from individual copies to whole shipments of thousands of copies.

Naturally, a wholesale price is going to be lower than a retail price. Let's suppose a book called *International Business* is on sale for $19.95 (retail) and the wholesale price is $10. The wholesale buyer must purchase at least 1,000 copies at a time to purchase at the $10 price.

A person walks through the front door and buys one copy of the book. The price is $19.95. Simple enough. You ring up the sale, put the book in a bag, and put the money in the cash register.

Now the phone rings and another customer, in another city a hundred miles away, wants to buy a copy to be shipped by parcel post. Your price to him is higher than $19.95 because you have to wrap the book properly for mailing, send someone to the post office, and pay the parcel post costs. He gives you a credit card number by phone so payment is all taken care of. But your price to him may be $25.50 to cover your extra costs, time and trouble.

Suppose he doesn't want to wait for parcel post but must have the book tomorrow. He is willing to pay for express air service and gives you his account number so the express charges will be billed directly to him. You still charge more than $19.95 because you still have extra charges of packing, labeling, calling the express air service, etc. So you charge $25 to cover what is involved for you.

The many variables here also affect your wholesale book business. Your wholesale book business exports, so let's take a close look at that.

Ocean Freight Options

You may be asked to ship your books by ocean under any number of terms. Frequently used terms of sale in world trade are discussed beginning on page 38. Some additional ones exist, but it's unlikely you'll encounter them. If one comes up, your forwarder can define it for you. If you are really interested in full descriptions of terms of sale and all the technical details, you can obtain a copy of *Incoterms* from the International Chamber of Commerce (see Resource List) or many libraries.

A caution if you have been involved in domestic shipping (within the U.S.): The terms of sale detailed here are different. For domestic, stick with what you're used to. For international, stick with the ones we're about to discuss.

USING THE RIGHT TERMINOLOGY

Remember that the terminology used in this chapter, and throughout this book, is from the language of terms used internationally.

For business conducted entirely within the United States, terms are subject to rules such as the Uniform Commercial Code. In a domestic sale, "FOB," for example, can mean something quite different from what we're talking about here.

If you've been doing business domestically, take time to be doubly sure that what you are saying is what you mean in your international business correspondence.

Ex Works

The most basic terminology in international shipping is *Ex Works*, abbreviated EXW. Ex Works refers to the days when places of business were known as "works"—the blacksmith's works, the iron works, the goldsmith's works. The process was easy. You ordered goods and you picked them up when they were ready. Everything was handled right at the works.

EXW functions the same way. Let's say a customer is interested in buying 1,000 copies of your book, for which you give a wholesale price of $10,000, excluding shipping or other charges. Your customer in Japan is willing to arrange for pickup at your "works." Your price would be quoted as $10,000 EXW.

For this price, you are expected to:

- Print the books and pack them suitable for shipping, perhaps twenty to a carton.
- Have all fifty cartons securely stacked on a shipping pallet, banded and labeled.
- Have the books available for pickup at the time agreed.

TERMS OF SALE VERSUS TERMS OF PAYMENT

It's important to remember that these are two entirely different things.

Terms of Sale, having to do with the Incoterms, determine shipping, when title passes and so on.

Terms of Payment determine how payment will be made: prepayment, open account, and everything else in between.

You can have an EXW shipment (Terms of Sale) that can be prepaid, under a letter of credit, or payable thirty days after the goods are received (Terms of Payment).

You can have a letter of credit (Terms of Payment) that is FOB New York, CFR Tokyo or CIF Hong Kong (Terms of Sale).

This is the whole agreement. The customer will arrange for pickup and take them on his way. Since he is responsible for arranging for shipment, any risk of loss or damage beyond your warehouse door is exclusively his. This is the same as your picking up the washing machine at Large's Department Store. (And, note again, this has nothing to do with payment. That is another subject. This has to do with what goods are being transferred to whom under what circumstances and when.)

Free Carrier

Free Carrier means that you are responsible for printing the books and packing them, having them ready for shipment, and also loading them on board the truck or other carrier that the customer sends to make the pickup.

It is certainly not uncommon, or too much to ask, to request that the seller (shipper/exporter) load the merchandise. So you will be glad to do so when the truck comes, and you will charge nothing extra. In fact, your price, free carrier or FCA, as it's abbreviated, is the same as your price EXW—$10,000.

KEEPING EXW AND FCA STRAIGHT

The worldwide misunderstanding on the Incoterms is between EXW and FCA.

EXW (Ex Works) means that the goods are available at your location for the buyer to pick up and transport.

FCA (Free carrier) means that you will load the transport vehicle.

To most of the world, EXW is considered to mean that the shipper (exporter) will in fact load the vehicle. If your buyer expects this, don't get hung up on it or expect him to fly in to load the vehicle. Go ahead and do the loading and call it EXW.

Free Alongside Ship

Suppose that your customer has made arrangements for ocean shipment of his goods but would like you to transport them to the port for him. You will be glad to do that, but you will charge extra for that service. This is known as shipping *free alongside ship*, or FAS.

Suppose now that your "works" are in Phoenix, Arizona, which does not have a seaport, and your customer is making arrangements for shipment from Los Angeles, California. You either have to send your truck to Los Angeles to make the delivery or use a trucking company that offers service "for hire" between Phoenix and Los Angeles (a "common carrier"). Perhaps you have no freight that you can bring back from California. Rather than run your own truck empty on the way back, you would probably decide to arrange for shipment via common carrier. Even if you were in the Los Angeles area, you would still have a choice of running your own truck to make the pier delivery or using

a local common carrier.

If, as in this example, you are in Phoenix, you will charge $750 for arranging for transport of the goods to the port. This is your price FAS.

Once again, you are responsible for printing the books, packing them ready for shipment, labeling them, and loading them on the truck, but you are also responsible for paying the truck bill for the transportation to the port.

This may be to the pier, literally "alongside the ship," or it could be a warehouse in the Los Angeles area where the steamship line gathers small shipments like yours and consolidates them, bringing them to the actual pier at their expense in time for sailing. The point is that you will arrange for delivery of the goods to the point as instructed, and you will pay for that part of the transportation.

So FAS Los Angeles or Long Beach or New York or Galveston is another way to quote on export shipments.

Three important points:

1. In accepting the responsibility for transporting the goods to Los Angeles, you also accept responsibility for the goods themselves. If the goods are damaged on the way to Los Angeles, *your* goods have been damaged, *not* your customer's goods. You do not turn over title to the goods until they are accepted by the steamship line's agent in Los Angeles.

2. Because you are responsible for this extra cost, you are certain to include the cost in your quotation to the customer. If you are charging out an additional $750 for arranging inland transportation to the pier, that is, your FAS price is $750 more than your EXW or FCA price, then you spell that out for the customer early in the process. If the customer requests it, yes, you can do it. Here is your new price: $10,750. That way

there are no surprises later on.

3. Note that your FAS price is your price for making this delivery. But that doesn't necessarily mean that this is an exact reflection of your bill from the trucking company, that you are simply passing on the bill, dollar for dollar. You can do that, of course, and many shippers do. But just as many if not more shippers build in extra dollars for their extra trouble: calling for the pickup, completing the truck bill of lading, paying out the truck charges, *and* shouldering the extra responsibility for the goods for a period of time while they are in transit.

Free on Board Vessel

Suppose your customer requests that you make the actual arrangements for shipping by ocean, and you include these in your price. Now he is asking you for a quotation FOB vessel, or *free on board* vessel, which entails more expense for you and more responsibility.

In this instance, you are being asked to print the books, pack them ready for shipment, label them, load them on a truck, pay for the trucking to the port, *and* to pay two other expenses: (1) the TRC or *terminal receiving charges* (or *wharfage*), which the steamship line charges to load your goods on board the vessel; and (2) the freight forwarder's bill. When you agree to ship FOB vessel, you become responsible for this bill, so you also have the right to choose which forwarder you will use.

Most forwarders charge a basic fee, or forwarding fee, for their services and then add on other charges for expenses such as:

- Messenger service
- Faxes, telexes, phone calls
- Document preparation
- Legalization and consularization fees
- Ocean insurance (if desired)

A freight forwarder should be able to supply you with a printed price list upon request and a written estimate of what the charges will be for a specific shipment. This should be very close to the actual charges (unless something unforeseen happens, necessitating additional phone calls, faxes, etc.).

If your customer requests that you ship FOB vessel, at whatever port, it is crucial that you protect yourself from surprises by getting the written quotation of estimated charges from a freight forwarder before you do your quotation. I cannot overemphasize how important this is. For some countries, the importer will need a certificate of origin prepared, which usually only costs a few dollars. In some other countries, the certificate of origin, invoice and packing slip may all need to be approved by that country's consulate in the United States. And some consulates (for example, Argentina's, as of this writing) charge as much as three percent of the value of your invoice. This is called *consularization* or *legalization*, and causes no difficulty as long as the forwarder knows in advance that it will be needed so *you* know the cost in advance.

In this example, after determining your forwarder's fee and allowing for your extra time and trouble, you will charge an additional $400 for an FOB vessel quotation, or $11,150.

Usually, in quoting FOB vessel the port city is listed as FOB vessel, Los Angeles, or FOB New York. Be very careful if quoting FOB vessel because the charges can vary from port to port. From your "works" location, your inland freight costs will be very different if you ship from Los Angeles, Galveston or New York. Therefore, it is important to be specific.

Check with your forwarder, however, before being too specific. In dealing with letters of credit, which will not be uncommon, it is important that the instructions in the letter be carried out exactly. Difficulties can arise if you quote FOB vessel, Los Angeles, and the steamship line you need to use sails from Long Beach. In the sample pro forma invoice on page 51, I listed California Port, which gives flexibility. Quoting FOB U.S. Port gives maximum flexibility.

TERMS OF SALE AT A GLANCE
- *EXW - Ex Works*
- *FCA - free carrier*
- *FAS - free alongside ship*
- *FOB - free on board*
- *CFR - cost and freight*
- *CIF - cost, insurance and freight*
- *CIP - cost, insurance and freight paid (to inland city)*

Cost and Freight

Another request may come for a quotation CFR Yokohama (*cost and freight to Yoko-hama*). In this instance, your customer is requesting that you obtain the ocean freight quotation and build that into your quotation. So, in addition to taking all the steps above, and having the responsibility to pay for them, you are now undertaking to pay the ocean freight on a "prepaid" basis rather than shipping "ocean freight collect" as was the case in the earlier examples.

After obtaining a current ocean freight quotation from your forwarder of $3,850, you can quote CFR Yokohama at $15,000.

Abbreviations used in previous years were "C + F" or "C&F," which you will still see from time to time.

Cost, Insurance and Freight

If your customer requests CIF Yokohama, he is requesting that you quote *cost, insur-ance, and freight* to Yokohama. Essentially this is the same as CFR except that you are

taking out a marine insurance policy. Defi-nitely a good idea, marine insurance nor-mally can cover the inland portions of the shipment too—"house to house" from your EXW location to the receiving point.

You check with your forwarder and find that the insurance costs $200, so your new quotation is $15,200.

IMPORTERS: CONTROL YOUR COSTS

As an importer, you should avoid accepting a CIF quotation as a matter of course. On CIF, the exporter (seller) is arranging the freight, including insurance, but as the buyer you are ultimately paying for it.

Generally, asking for an EXW, FCA, FOB quotation, and then a CIF quotation puts you in a good situation to control costs.

When asking for the pro forma invoice, ask for the weight and dimensions as well. This enables you to go to your freight forwarder and inquire about inbound freight rates yourself.

Perhaps the exporter is marking up the CIF quotation for extra profit, hasn't shopped for the best rates, or simply hasn't contacted the carrier that your forwarder works with.

By having your own freight quotation, you have the option of arranging transportation yourself on an EXW, FCA or FOB basis if your costs will be cheaper.

If you use a letter of credit, specify the car-rier to be used. ("Full set of clean on board bills of lading from XYZ Steamship Lines.")

As to insurance, your forwarder can easily set it up for you from your end.

Microbridge Service

Another possibility exists. Suppose your customer is in the city of Kozu, which is somewhat inland. He requests that you pro-vide a quote CIP Kozu which means *cost, freight and insurance paid to Kozu*. Here, you are being asked to:

- Manufacture the goods and pack them ready for shipment
- Transport them to the pier, or to wherever the steamship line designates
- Make arrangements with the freight forwarder
- Pay the ocean freight
- Arrange for insurance
- Arrange for shipment inland

Is it indeed possible for you to arrange inland transportation in Japan for your customer and arrange delivery to his inland city? Yes, it is. Some steamship lines offer *microbridge service* to provide for this.

You pay an additional amount for the extra carriage to the inland city, and the customer arranges for customs clearance in Japan and final delivery.

In this case, you find that microbridge service is available to Kozu for an additional $300, and so you quote to your customer: CIP Kozu, $15,500.

Microbridge service exists *from* as well as *to* many inland points in the United States. You export goods FOB Des Moines, St. Louis and Dallas as easily as from Los Angeles or New York. Also, you can import goods to inland cities without having to bother with making your arrangements yourself to clear customs at the ocean port or to truck your goods from the port to your city. In chapter ten, you will see how many medium to large inland U.S. cities have service through microbridges and an incredibly valuable hybrid called the *non-vessel operating common carrier* (NVOCC).

Think Insurance

I always recommend that a shipment be insured, because you are the owner of the goods until title passes, whether at your door, at the pier, once on board the vessel, or (in CFR, CIF and CIP) until the shipment reaches destination.

In some cases, your customer may tell you that he does not want you to purchase insurance because he already has a blanket cargo policy that he buys each year to cover all his import shipments. Or, as you expand, you may buy a blanket policy to cover all your shipments. But it is extremely important under all circumstances that an insurance policy be bought on the shipment.

Air and Ground Transportation

Most of the processes and terminology for ocean shipments also apply to shipments transported via aircraft, rail or truck. Here is a quick look at how these variables work for air and ground shipments.

Air Freight

- EXW is the same term: from your "works."
- FCA is also the same term; you are loading the truck.
- FAS air carrier is similar to FAS vessel. You are responsible for delivering the goods to the airport, as directed by the air freight forwarder, usually to his terminal or an airline terminal. Even though we are dealing with an aircraft here, the abbreviation is still FAS.
- FOB airport (FOB Chicago, FOB Salt Lake City) indicates that you will produce and pack the goods, deliver them to the airport, pay the forwarder, and be responsible for any loading charges. The shipment will go air freight collect.
- CFR airport (CFR Yokohama, CFR Tokyo, CFR Kozu) means you will pay all the charges, including the air freight.
- CIF airport (CIF Yokohama, CIF Tokyo, CIF Kozu) is again, the same as CFR, plus insurance.

You normally won't see CIP in air freight

because the CFR and CIF designations can cover the shipment to an inland airport.

Ground Transportation

For ground transportation (rail and truck), as with air freight, CIP is also generally not used. So the typical terms of sale are:

- *EXW Denver*—exactly the same; from your "works."
- *FCA Denver*—does not exist because FOB Denver in this case is the same thing.
- *FOB Denver*—you load the truck or rail car in the city where the shipment originates, rather than going to a seaport.
- *CFR Toronto*—you load the truck in the city where the shipment originates and pay the freight all the way to Toronto.
- *CIF Toronto*—you load the truck in the origin city, pay the freight costs all the way to Toronto and insure the shipment.

In some cases, your customer may ask you to quote DAF, or *delivered at frontier* Buffalo or DAF Laredo (the border crossing), after which the shipment is your consignee's responsibility. Sometimes this is quoted as CFR Buffalo or CFR Laredo, but that is not technically correct.

ON AIR INSURANCE

Most airlines offer insurance on their air waybill. Be aware that this does not create an insurance certificate. If you are working with a letter of credit requiring insurance, ask your forwarder to obtain independent cargo insurance coverage that gives you a certificate to present to the bank.

For the Importer

The same Incoterms apply in reverse when you import goods. For example:

- EXW Paris
- FAS Le Havre (port city)
- FOB Le Havre
- CFR New York City
- CIF New York City
- CIP Hackensack, New Jersey

OCEAN—TERMS OF SALE

TERMS OF SALE	EXPORTER'S ROLE	BUYER ASSUMES POSSESSION AT
EXW—Ex Works	Goods packed, labeled, ready to go	Exporter's "works"
FCA—Free Carrier	Prepare goods, load truck	Exporter's "works"
FAS—Free Alongside Ship	Ship to port, pay truck freight	The vessel, port city
FOB—Free On Board	Ship to port, on board vessel, pay forwarder	The vessel, port city
CFR—Cost and Freight CIF*—Cost, Insurance and Freight	Ship to destination port	Destination port
CIP*—Cost, Insurance Paid to	Pay freight to inland point at destination	Inland point
* Exporter pays insurance		

AIR—TERMS OF SALE

TERMS OF SALE	EXPORTER'S ROLE	BUYER ASSUMES POSSESSION AT
EXW—Ex Works	Goods packed, labeled, ready to go	Exporter's "works"
FCA—Free Carrier	Prepare goods, load truck	Exporter's "works"
FAS—Free Alongside Ship	Ship to airport, pay truck freight	The airport
FOB—Free On Board	Ship to airport, on board aircraft, pay forwarder	The aircraft, airport city
CFR—Cost and Freight CIF*—Cost, Insurance and Freight	Pay freight to airport at destination city	Destination airport
* Exporter pays insurance		

GROUND (TRUCK, RAIL)—TERMS OF SALE

TERMS OF SALE	EXPORTER'S ROLE	BUYER ASSUMES POSSESSION AT
EXW—Ex Works	Goods packed, labeled, ready to go	Exporter's "works"
FOB—Free On Board	Prepare goods, load truck	Exporter's "works"
DAF—Delivered At Frontier	Ship to border, pay truck freight	National border at named border point
CFR—Cost and Freight CIF*—Cost, Insurance and Freight	Pay freight to destination city in foreign country	Destination city
* Exporter pays insurance		

CHAPTER SIX

The Pro Forma Invoice

- *Spelling Out the Specifics*

- *Refining the Quote*

- *Communicating Via the Pro Forma Invoice*

A pro forma invoice is your quotation for the goods you are offering to ship. The name comes from the Latin, *pro forma*, "in the form of" an invoice.

If you are exporting, you will be asked for a pro forma invoice. If you are importing, you should ask for it as you proceed with planning your order.

SPELLING OUT THE SPECIFICS

Good negotiating results in agreement on three things: goods, price and terms. Start with the goods—what you are selling or buying. Spell out colors, quantities and any special features so both parties have in black and white exactly what is being bought and sold. If this is done properly, no one has any doubts, and a customer does not receive 100 items instead of 1,000 in the wrong color or the wrong size.

The pro forma invoice and an appropriate cover letter are probably the most important documents an exporter prepares. The pro forma invoice should be thorough enough to cover all the relevant details. It is much better to have the buyer fax now and say, "No, that's not what I wanted," than to find out later when the goods are in his warehouse that there has been a misunderstanding.

Pro Forma Invoice Vs. Export Price List

Business people outside the United States sometimes ask for a "pro forma invoice for your widgets, giving us best export price." In this case, the customer doesn't really want a pro forma invoice yet but a copy of your export price list, showing EXW prices for various products you sell. From the export price list, the importer can determine the actual costs of your goods in any combination.

Send the export price list with your regular catalog or other descriptive material. Ideally, you have one set of advertising material you give everyone, with a separate price page for export. This keeps down the amount of printing you have to pay for and keep track of.

WHAT IS THE PRO FORMA INVOICE?

The pro forma invoice is a quotation, subject to the importer's (buyer's) approval. Every time you've obtained a written quotation in your business or personal life, you've obtained the equivalent of a pro forma invoice.

The letter of credit is set up in accordance with the pro forma invoice.

If you leave something out of a pro forma invoice that is important to you (last shipping date, expiration date for the letter of credit, whether or not it includes legalized documents), the letter of credit may have a clause that you find difficult or impossible to accept.

Amending a letter of credit is not always simple. You may have to start negotiating all over again. The buyer may have assumed things to be a certain way and get upset that you're trying to change things around after the deal is made.

Before issuing a pro forma invoice, faxes should be going back and forth to clarify exactly what the deal is and what the letter of credit should say on key points.

List definite dates during which your export price list is effective. With normal inflation, you will increase your prices as time goes on. Someone you wrote to in 1992 may contact you in 1997 seeking to order. The export price list he has is obviously out of date; it says so itself. The price list can also speed up orders toward expiration date, as customers anticipating a price increase rush in a final order.

However you set up the export price list, remember that from that point until the list's expiration it will be very difficult to increase the price. You can only go down. It is extremely important to leave a little "fat" in these prices. Many importers, upon receiving your prices, will contact you asking for a further concession. By quoting prices just a few percentage points above what you really are willing to sell for, you have something left to "give away" if you need to. And if you don't need to, so much the better.

Using Price Lists Effectively

Export Price List Example A on page 48 shows the list price (retail) for the merchandise, to give the importer an idea of what the items sell for to the consumer so he can plan his markup. USD means U.S. dollars to avoid confusion with Canadian dollars and Mexican pesos, which, along with U.S. dollars, are often abbreviated "$." (Infrequently, USC is used for *United States currency*.)

A percentage discount is given, based on how large the order is. In this case, the discount applies to any product or mixture of products, assuming a minimum of USD 2,500 per order. After all, this is wholesale.

Of course, you can also list products at a given wholesale price, as in Export Price List Example B, page 49. Some of your products may have markups quite different from others. Rather than offering the same percent discount from retail on every item, you may be able to be more competitive by discounting some items more drastically than others.

Notice that at the bottom of both price lists, the terms and conditions of sale are explained:

1. Terms and conditions for payment are clearly stated:

    a) at sight (not time), meaning payment is made "at sight" of documents, not on extended terms

    b) letter of credit (not a draft alone)

    c) in U.S. dollars (not the importer's country's currency)

    d) on a U.S. bank (to be payable here)

Ideally, you want a confirmed letter of credit, and you may want to ask for it here. However, whether or not a letter of credit will be confirmed is ultimately a decision made by the advising bank

2. The alternative of a 2 percent discount from the merchandise amount is offered if the customer prepays in U.S. dollars payable at a U.S. bank.

It is clear (line 4) that the discount applies only to the EXW amount—the merchandise itself. If you are not precise on this point, your customer might take a 2 percent discount from the CIF amount of USD 14,200, which would mean a discount of USD 284. Do not discount the freight costs here because you have to lay those out regardless; you only discount the cost of the merchandise itself.

3. Bankers are listed. Ideally, a letter of credit will be advised through that bank, although it depends on which international banker your customer uses and who the U.S. correspondent bank is. But if need be, you can call your bank into the transaction later on anyway (see next chapter).

4. All prices are ex works. This makes it clear that no shipping costs or insurance are covered at these prices.

5. Export packing is included. Depending on the goods, packing may be more involved and more expensive for an export shipment, primarily for perishables, hazardous materials, or very fragile or very expensive commodities. This case deals with merchandise for which the regular packing will

---

EXPORT PRICE LIST EXAMPLE A

(See product descriptions in enclosed catalog.)

Universal Exports
1700 West Washington Street
Phoenix, AZ 85007 U.S.A.
Telephone: (602) 555-1212
Telefax: (602) 555-5555

BOOKS:

International Business	List	USD	20.00
Importing Ideas	List	USD	15.00
International Statistics	List	USD	50.00
How to Be a Freight Forwarder	List	USD	20.00

OFFICE SUPPLIES:

A400 Universal Calculator	List	USD	5.00
A500 Universal Calculator	List	USD	10.00
A600 Pencil Sharpener	List	USD	10.00
Widgets	List	USD	5.00

EXPORT DISCOUNTS:

Minimum USD 2,500 order	25% discount
Minimum USD 5,000 order	50% discount
Minimum USD 15,000 order	55% discount

EFFECTIVE: August 1, 1995
EXPIRES: July 31, 1996

TERMS AND CONDITIONS:
Sight letter of credit in U.S. Dollars on a U.S. Bank
2% additional discount for advance payment in U.S. Dollars (check payable at a U.S. Bank)
Our Bankers: State National Bank, Phoenix, AZ, U.S.A.
All prices Ex Works Phoenix, AZ, U.S.A.
Export Packing Included

be sufficient so nothing extra is charged. Any extra charges, such as for special export packing, are normally included in the EXW price; this fact is stated here so everyone is quite clear as to what is required.

After your customer studies an export price list, and perhaps asks for a sample (which you may send by airmail free, or charge full list price for, depending on what the sample is worth and the practice in your industry), he or she will ask for a pro forma invoice, which should say "pro forma invoice for your product, quantity 1,000." In this case, the customer has selected a textbook.

REFINING THE QUOTE

What terms of sale are you quoting—FCA or CFR or CIF? Your quotation will be quite different for each of these options. Air or

EXPORT PRICE EXAMPLE B

(See product descriptions in enclosed catalog.)

Universal Exports
1700 West Washington Street
Phoenix, AZ 85007 U.S.A.
Telephone: (602) 555-1212
Telefax: (602) 555-5555

BOOKS:	Retail	10+	20+	50+
International Business	USD 20	17	15	13
Importing Ideas	USD 15	13	12	10
International Statistics	USD 50	40	35	30
How to Be a Freight Forwarder	USD 20	17	15	13
OFFICE SUPPLIES:				
A400 Universal Calculator	USD 5	4	3	2.50
A500 Universal Calculator	USD 10	8	7	6
A600 Pencil Sharpener	USD 10	8	7	6
Widgets	USD 5	4	3	2.50

EFFECTIVE: August 1, 1995
EXPIRES: July 31, 1996

TERMS AND CONDITIONS:
Sight letter of credit in U.S. Dollars on a U.S. Bank
2% additional discount for advance payment in U.S. Dollars (check payable at a U.S. Bank)
Our Bankers: State National Bank, Phoenix, AZ, U.S.A.
All prices Ex Works Phoenix, AZ, U.S.A.
Export Packing Included

ocean? How are you going to set up this shipment? When does the customer need the product? Do you have ninety days to ship or will you have to put everyone on overtime to get the order out next week?

How will the customer pay you? Letter of credit? Sight draft? Does he think you are going to ship on a time draft? Will he prepay you in U.S. dollars on a U.S. bank and thus be eligible for your discount?

In many cases, the importer is not very clear about what he wants. He may not be sure himself how he wants the shipment handled. He will leave it to you to come back with a pro forma that is acceptable to him.

Actually, this does not put you in a bad situation. When you reply with your pro forma, fill in all the details. One of the rules of negotiating is that once you put something in it is up to the other side to negotiate it back out.

If the importer is not specific, you should reply with a pro forma specifying:

- FCA Phoenix, Arizona, U.S.A. (If you can move it FCA, it is very easy for you. If the importer wants it another way, he will ask for it.)

- Air or ocean (depending primarily on size and value of the shipment).
- Sight letter of credit, naming your local international bank (more about letters of credit in the next chapter), or prepayment with a discount for paying in advance if it is a very small order.
- Shipping time: thirty days, sixty days, ninety days, from receipt of letter of credit, depending on the time frame you need. Basing it on the time from receipt of the letter of credit means that you will not start production until the letter of credit is received. (If the importer changes his mind, you are not stuck with having bought too much raw material, etc.)

In the Pro Forma Invoice Model on page 51, you can easily see the progression of the quotation as your responsibility for charges becomes more extensive.

Normally you would not quote seven possible prices to your customer, since this tends to confuse the issue. You normally quote at most two prices: EXW, and the shipping terms he requested. I always prefer to list the EXW price for the merchandise on a pro forma invoice so no one forgets the price of the merchandise itself as we discuss additional charges.

The customer might ask you for FCA and CIF, or FOB vessel East, Gulf, or West Coast Port, and CFR, so she can look at the cost options of your routing versus what she is able to find.

The most common request you will receive is "give us your best export prices, CIF our port, for. . . ."

Suppose your customer asks for a CIF quotation. You prepare a pro forma invoice as in the pro forma invoice example on page 51. Here, we have the one CIF quote to Yokohama, and we have added some terms and conditions to help outline what we, as

the exporters, need. Most are familiar from the export price list.

CLARIFY THE DETAILS

Before issuing the pro forma invoice, make sure you clarify the following points with your buyer:

1. *Final shipping date.*
2. *Expiration date of letter of credit.*
3. *Other deadlines, if any, that are important to the buyer.*
4. *What documents are needed.*
5. *Special inspections or certifications involved.*
6. *Specific packing or labeling requirements.*

Establishing a Time Frame

An important component of the pro forma invoice is the establishment of a time frame. Take a look under "Terms and Conditions" on the pro forma invoice example.

These terms and conditions include three issues of timing:

1. A statement that the price is good for ninety days. You cannot be expected to hold one price open forever, and sometimes this helps speed up an order at this stage.

2. A statement that you can ship within sixty days after receipt of the letter of credit or prepayment. You may need to indicate forty-five days or ninety days, depending on the time you need to get together raw materials, manufacture the product and ship it. This way, you do not manufacture your product, possibly with special labeling or user instructions in a foreign language, that you cannot use in the United States, and then have the product tied up in your warehouse.

What if it takes two months for the letter of credit to come through? What if the buyer changes his mind? I recommend, at least until you have had several orders from

PRO FORMA INVOICE MODEL

FROM: Universal Exports
1700 West Washington Street
Phoenix, AZ 85007 U.S.A.

TO: Japan Imports
147 Chuo-Ku
Yokohama, Japan

DATE: September 1, 1995

1,000 (one thousand) copies of International Business @ USD 10.00	USD 10,000.00
EXW Phoenix, AZ (Ex Works)	USD 10,000.00
FCA Phoenix, AZ (Free Carrier)	USD 10,000.00
FAS California Port (Free Alongside Ship)	USD 10,150.00
FOB California Port (Free on Board)	USD 10,350.00
CFR Yokohama (Cost and Freight)	USD 11,000.00
CIF Yokohama (Cost, Insurance and Freight)	USD 11,075.00
CIP Kozu (Cost, Insurance and Freight Paid)	USD 11,500.00

PRO FORMA INVOICE EXAMPLE

FROM: Universal Exports
1700 West Washington Street
Phoenix, AZ 85007 U.S.A.

TO: Japan Imports
147 Chuo-Ku
Yokohama, Japan

DATE: September 1, 1995

1,000 (one thousand) copies of International Business, @ USD 10.00	
EXW Phoenix, AZ, U.S.A.	USD 10,000.00
CIF Yokohama (Cost, Insurance and Freight)	USD 11,075.00

TERMS AND CONDITIONS:
Sight letter of credit in U.S. Dollars on a U.S. Bank
2% additional discount from EXW cost ($200) for advance payment in U.S. Dollars (check payable at a U.S. Bank)
Our Bankers: State National Bank, Phoenix, AZ, U.S.A.
Export Packing Included
Prices Good for 90 days
Shipment: Within 60 days after receipt of check or letter of credit. Please open letter of credit for 90 days total.
Thank you.

one customer and you know each other well, that you do not put the order together until the letter of credit is in hand and you, your banker and your forwarder all agree that it is satisfactory.

Requesting the time you need to manufacture the goods and have them ready for shipment means you do not have to start until then, and there is one less way you can get burned.

3. A request of ninety days total to ship under the letter of credit. This is in case:

    a) There is a delay getting materials or producing the goods.

    b) Vessels are overbooked, or you miss the intended vessel.

    c) You need time to get documents together under the letter of credit.

In other words, as any Boy Scout knows, "Be prepared." If your time frame permits everything to go on time only if everything goes smoothly, something will go wrong.

The exact time frame you should request varies depending on your particular needs and the advice of your freight forwarder. (Do the vessels sail weekly or monthly to this particular destination?)

By being as specific as possible on these points when you issue the pro forma invoice, you avoid problems later.

CHECKLIST FOR PRO FORMA INVOICE

    1. Description of product
    2. Price
    3. Terms of sale
    4. Terms of payment
    5. Length of time prices are valid
    6. Length of time needed for shipping

Documentation

As we will see in chapter eight, some countries require special certificates of origin and/or legalization or consularization of documents. Some products going to some countries may require particular certification (food, pharmaceutical products).

Your customer is the best person to know what documents will be required by Customs or other agencies in his country. Ordinarily, he will bring this up when he asks for a pro forma invoice. ("Please note that legalization of documents by our consulate is required.") If the issue has not been raised, and your forwarder indicates that special documentation is required, now is the time for *you* to bring it up. Otherwise, it will suddenly appear as a requirement in the letter of credit, and you will not have the costs for it covered in your quotation.

If specialized documentation *may* be required in a particular instance, and it has not been requested, you should note on the pro forma invoice that the price *does not* include the documentation. In a cover letter, clearly point this out again to your customer and ask him to notify you if the documentation is in fact required. This gives him a chance to get back to you with the information before everything is cast in stone.

If your customer has not asked for special documents and then answers you that, yes, he does need them, it does not mean he was trying to trick you. A textile product importer in a country that requires import licenses and legalized documents for all textile products may assume that is the way the whole world works. (Remember ethnocentrism. The importer will assume that you need legalization to bring textiles into the United States—even though you do not—and that you will automatically know it's needed and allow for it.)

COMMUNICATING VIA THE PRO FORMA INVOICE

Communication is very important. The pro forma invoice is normally your final opportunity to communicate inexpensively before letters of credit are issued.

When sending a pro forma, I usually send a cover sheet thanking the customer for the order and also asking when payment is to be sent or the letter of credit opened. For example: "Please advise name of opening bank and letter of credit number." Since the letter of credit number is not available to the customer until the letter of credit is actually opened, this gives you advance notice that a letter of credit has in fact been opened and is now on the way to you. Special requirements for the letter of credit should be noted here, too.

The important thing is to discuss all aspects of the sale and come to an agreement *before* payment is sent and or before a letter of credit is issued.

CHAPTER SEVEN

The Ins and Outs of Getting Paid

- *The Letter of Credit*
- *Time Letters of Credit and Time Drafts*
- *Direct Payment*
- *Cash Against Documents*

A gain, let me give you my magic formula (previously discussed in chapter one) for successful export transactions:

1. Get the order.
2. Make sure you are going to get paid for the order.
3. Ship the order.

Always work in this sequence; never put number three ahead of number two.

THE LETTER OF CREDIT

The accepted methods of payment in international trade have developed over hundreds of years to provide protection to both the seller and the buyer. Letters of credit (also sometimes known as *documentary credits*) are an important method of payment.

The transaction protects both the importer and the exporter. In the sample transaction later in this chapter, the importer is in Japan, Japan Imports, and the exporter is in the United States, Universal Exports, as on the pro forma invoice. The transaction works like this:

1. The importer goes to her international bank and applies for a letter of credit for, say, USD 14,200. The bank satisfies itself that the importer is good for the funds. If the bank deems it necessary, it may freeze the USD 14,200 in the importer's account until it is payable.

2. The importer advises her international bank of the documents she will require from the exporter. For example:

a) Full set of clean, on-board, ocean bills of lading, issued "to order"

b) Commercial invoice, original and five copies

c) Packing slip, original and five copies

d) Insurance certificates (on a CIF shipment)

(I will go over these documents, but for right now, take my word for it that these are typical documents on an ocean shipment, and they are not at all complicated.)

Since the importer applies for the letter of credit, she is sometimes called the *applicant*. Since she opens the letter of credit through her bank, she is sometimes called the *opener*.

3. The bank puts the requirements into letter form and sends the letter to a bank in the exporter's country. This may be transmitted by mail, telex, or a system operated specifically for international banking, called SWIFT (Society for Worldwide Interbank Financial Transactions). This bank is called the *opening* or *originating* bank.

4. The bank in the United States sends the original letter of credit to the exporter. This bank is known as the *advising bank*, advising the letter of credit to the exporter.

5. The exporter manufactures the product and ships, *in such a way as to comply exactly with the letter of credit*. This means all the documents must be prepared exactly as outlined in the letter of credit. And, if specified, particular ports or steamship lines called for by the importer in the letter of credit must be used.

6. Following shipment, the documents proving that shipment was made, and made in conformance with the letter of credit, are sent or delivered to the U.S. bank.

7. The U.S. bank receives funds from the importer's bank and pays the exporter, commonly known as the *beneficiary* of the letter of credit. The importer's bank has secure funds from the importer from the time when the letter of credit was first opened.

While this is going on, the documents are sent to the importer's bank for ultimate delivery to the importer in exchange for the funds that are now in the exporter's hands. What has happened is that the banks have taken the place of exporter and importer in exchanging the documents on the shipment and the money.

Once the letter of credit has been issued, the importer cannot change her mind or amend the letter of credit unless the exporter agrees (more about amendments on pages 62-63), so the exporter can feel confident that as soon as she ships with all the documentation in order, she will be paid. At the same time, the importer knows that the exporter cannot get the money until she ships the goods.

As far as the banks are concerned, the letter of credit is the final word on the transaction. It does not matter what you and the other party have agreed to if it is not reflected in the letter of credit. So it is important, in dealing with letters of credit, that everyone knows exactly what everyone else needs before the letter of credit is issued, not just before shipment is made. Amendments can be made, but they cost money at both the opener's end and at the beneficiary's end.

HOW TO REQUEST A LETTER OF CREDIT FROM AN IMPORTER

Before you request that a buyer provide you with a letter of credit, you need to know what to look for. You'll need to:

1. *Know who should be the advising (U.S.) bank.*
2. *Know how long you'll have to ship after the letter of credit arrives.*
3. *Know how much time you'll need to present documents.*
4. *Make sure the letter of credit is irrevocable.*
5. *Make sure it's payable at sight.*
6. *Establish that the exporter (beneficiary) will pay U.S. banking charges and the importer (applicant) will pay*

banking charges in his country.
7. *Spell out any special requirements.*

Once the letter of credit is opened, make sure you're advised of the name of the opening bank and the letter of credit number.

IMPORTER'S LETTER OF CREDIT CHECKLIST

As an importer, ask these questions when opening a letter of credit.

1. *Is it to be confirmed?*
2. *What are your banking charges?*
3. *Is it payable in U.S. dollars?*
4. *How much time will you allow to ship?*
5. *How much time will you allow to present documents?*
6. *What documents are required?*
7. *Is it in accordance with the pro forma invoice (i.e., is this what you agreed to)?*
8. *What shipping requirements will you provide (specific steamship line, etc.)?*

Understanding the Letter of Credit

Read through the following letter of credit, and then we'll study it in detail.

The Opening

Let's look at the first sentence of the sample, a complex statement packed with important information:

By order of Japan Imports, Yokohama, Japan, we advise this irrevocable Documentary Credit number 4129 in favor of Universal Exports, Phoenix, AZ, U.S.A. for the amount of USD 11,075.00 (Eleven thousand, seventy-five and 00/100 United States Dollars) available at sight, against your drafts, accompanied by the following documents:

LETTER OF CREDIT

Their Ref: 4129   Our Ref: 7268 P

State National Bank   November 15, 1995
Phoenix, AZ

By order of Japan Imports, Yokohama, Japan, we advise this irrevocable Documentary Credit number 4129 in favor of Universal Exports, Phoenix, AZ, U.S.A. for the amount of USD 11,075.00 (Eleven thousand, seventy-five and 00/100 United States Dollars) available at sight, against your drafts, accompanied by the following documents:

Full set of clean on board bills of lading issued to order of shipper, marked notify applicant, freight prepaid.

Beneficiary's signed commercial invoices in original and five copies.

Packing slip in original and five copies.

Certificate of origin in two copies, notarized and approved by the Chamber of Commerce.

Insurance policy in negotiable form issued to our order and showing claims payable at destination for the full invoice amount plus 10% covering All Risks, S.R.C.C., war clause.

For: 1,000 textbooks per pro forma invoice dated September 1, 1995.

Shipment From: West Coast U.S.A. port

Shipment To: Yokohama, Japan

Shipment Not Later Than: March 31, 1996

Date of Expiry: April 15, 1996

Part Shipments: Prohibited

Transshipments: Permitted

Documents must be presented within ten days after shipment.
Banking charges in the United States for the account of beneficiary. Applicant's bank: First Bank of Yokohama.

We hereby confirm this letter of credit.

Glenna Hathaway

for State National Bank

Make sure your letter of credit clearly indicates "irrevocable" somewhere on the document. This means that it cannot be revoked before the expiry date. (On the expiry date, if documents have not been presented, the letter of credit of course expires by itself.)

A "revocable" letter of credit could be revoked by the opener anytime he felt like it. For example, the opener could revoke the letter of credit the day after you ship but before you have been able to present documents to the bank, so the documents and the shipment would be in limbo and you would not get paid.

Frankly, I have never seen a revocable letter of credit. But if I did see one, I would never ship under it under any circumstances.

In the sample letter of credit, the first paragraph is a summary of the transaction. It names the applicant, the beneficiary, and the amount of the letter of credit. The letter also says "payable at sight against your drafts."

A *draft* is similar in format to a check, and your forwarder has blanks. You can also buy them yourself from sources you will find in the Resource List located on pages 145-147. This is like writing a check to yourself from your customer. The banks need a document on which to make payment. The letter of credit refers to *drafts* (plural) because you submit the draft in duplicate.

At sight means that you are paid immediately, or after the bank has had an opportunity to review the documents and make sure everything conforms to the letter of credit's requirements.

Next the letter of credit specifies the documents that must be presented in accordance with the letter of credit, as discussed above.

Full set of clean on board bills of lading issued to order of shipper, marked notify applicant, freight prepaid.

Bills of lading are the documents issued by a steamship line, an airline, a railroad or a trucking company (the "carrier"), summarizing the shipment. *On board*, a term used by steamship lines, means that the carrier is certifying that the goods are indeed "on board" the ship. This makes it clear that the steamship line has not merely accepted the cargo for a ship scheduled to sail next Saturday. It is on board the ship, and the sailing date is listed. "On board" bills of lading are not issued until after the ship has sailed.

Full set tells us again that this is an ocean shipment, since this phrase only occurs in ocean shipping. Steamship lines usually issue three original bills of lading, signed by the captain or someone on his behalf. The letter of credit requires that all the originals be presented to the bank. That constitutes a full set.

Three nonnegotiable copies of the ocean bill of lading are generally required. These are simply file copies, clearly stamped "nonnegotiable" and not signed. When the three original bills of lading are sent, plenty of nonnegotiables are sent along so everyone who needs a copy can have one.

Notice that the letter of credit says "to order of shipper." This makes each of the original bills of lading the title to the cargo as far as the steamship line is concerned. Imagine if the deed to your house or the title to your car were made out to "bearer," and whoever got hold of the original document could claim ownership!

LETTERS OF CREDIT: GUARANTEED PAYMENT?

A letter of credit is not, *no matter what anyone tells you, a guarantee that you will be paid. A letter of credit is a guarantee that the buyer's bank will pay as long as the letter of credit is conformed to exactly. If there is one error or omission in your documentation, then you are paid only if the buyer decides to excuse it.*

If a letter of credit is confirmed, then the U.S. advising bank is guaranteeing payment if everything is done perfectly.

Other Terms and Clauses

The rest of the letter of credit is easy to understand because we have already gone over most of these aspects.

Beneficiary's signed commercial invoices in original and five copies.

Signed commercial invoice is the same invoice you see every day. The importer is asking you to sign the original before sending it to the bank and include five copies. It is not unusual at all for an importer to request a signed copy. Some customs offices require it, and it is traditional anyway.

I like to use the phrase, "This is to certify that this is a true and correct invoice," and then sign it. My certification is that I have personally gone over it and approved it, and it tends to make everyone more comfortable than "just" a signature.

And, if the goods are made in the United States, I use: "This is to certify that this is a true and correct invoice, and that these goods were manufactured in the United States of America."

Packing slip in original and five copies.

This is simple enough. It is your ordinary packing slip. You may already be using a multipart form that prepares a packing slip when you do your invoice.

Certificate of origin in two copies issued by the Chamber of Commerce.

Easy to obtain (see chapter eight).

Insurance policy in negotiable form issued to our order and showing claims payable at destination for the full invoice amount plus 10% covering All Risks, S.R.C.C., war clause.

A maritime insurance policy can be issued directly to someone or "to order." Under a letter of credit with negotiable bills, a negotiable insurance policy is quite common. This policy is for All Risks, S.R.C.C. (strikes, riots and civil commotions) and war risk.

Whole books have been written about maritime insurance. Suffice it to say that these three clauses are the most common on letters of credit (and non-letter-of-credit shipments) that I have seen. This way, you have good coverage for a nominal fee.

Make sure the coverage is issued "door-to-door," which provides insurance from your building (EXW location) to the importer's building, even while the goods are on a truck to or from the pier.

Where do you get the insurance? Your freight forwarder can arrange it for you.

for: 1,000 textbooks per Pro Forma Invoice dated September 1, 1995.

This is a brief description of the goods to be shipped, citing the pro forma invoice, which had all the details. You are to ship in accordance with what you agreed to on the pro forma invoice.

On each document you submit to the bank, type the phrase "1,000 books per Pro Forma Invoice dated September 1, 1995."

Shipment From: West Coast U.S.A. port

Remember from chapter five why we wanted it this way.

Shipment To: Yokohama, Japan

This shows the port to which the bills of lading show the cargo being shipped.

Shipment Not Later Than: March 31, 1996

This is the latest possible date you are allowed to ship, and in this letter of credit it means the sailing date. If the ship sails one day later, you have a discrepancy in the letter of credit and may not get paid.

Murphy's Law applies: Wait until the last minute for a ship that sails March 31, 1996, and watch the ship be delayed to April 1, 1996 (April Fool's Day). March 31, 1996 is a Sunday, but vessels do sail on Sundays.

Date of Expiry: April 15, 1996

This is the date the letter of credit expires. No matter what, you must get the documents to the advising bank by April 15, 1996. As with your tax return, April 15 is OK; April 16 is no good. If you submit the documents after the expiration, there is no longer a letter of credit to pay you.

Part Shipments: Prohibited

The importer does not want you to send part shipments (which would result in multiple entries at his customs office and delays and expense for him). Send it all at once. That saves you money, as well as bother, because one large shipment usually costs less than several small shipments.

Part shipments may be authorized if, for example, your importer wanted 1,000 books shipped every month for a year. To maximize cash flow, he may want to have a chance to sell each 1,000 before the next 1,000 arrives. The bank may have enough of his money frozen to cover the entire letter of credit, but it may be in an interest-bearing account.

Transshipments: Prohibited

In true transshipment cargo is shipped to a destination, unloaded, and a new shipment begins with a new bill of lading. This type of transshipment is generally prohibited in a letter of credit because it is easy to lose control of cargo. (I will discuss more about transshipments on pages 101-102.) The importer wants through service to Yokohama.

Documents must be presented within ten days after shipment.

It is not uncommon for an importer to request that documents be presented quickly. Here, you have ten days after the date of sailing. Service is so quick (Los Angeles to Tokyo in fourteen days) that the importer wants a chance to have the documents needed to claim ("to order" original bills of lading) and clear customs (invoice, packing slips) before he has to pay storage charges at the steamship line.

Of course, it is a matter of routine to present the documents as quickly as possible, not only out of fairness to the customer, but because the quicker you present the documents, the quicker you get paid!

If nothing is mentioned in the letter of credit about the time required to present documents, you have twenty-one days.

Banking charges in the United States for the account of beneficiary. Applicant's bank: First Bank of Yokohama.

You pay your advising bank's charges, and the importer pays the charges of the bank in Japan. This is normal; sometimes one party picks up all the charges. The bank will usually wait for payment and deduct its charges before paying you.

We hereby confirm this letter of credit.

Last is one of the most important clauses. A letter of credit can be confirmed by your bank. In this instance the U.S. bank is taking the place of the foreign bank in guaranteeing payment.

On a confirmed letter of credit, "at sight," you are paid by the U.S. bank no matter what happens to the importer (applicant) or even his bank (opening bank) as long as you have conformed exactly to the letter of credit.

Regardless of wars, revolutions or bankruptcies elsewhere, you have only to look to your international banker for payment.

Publication 500: The Letter of Credit Handbook

So where am I getting all this? From "Documentary Credits," Publication 500 of the International Chamber of Commerce. The ICC is the same group that publishes the *Incoterms* book referred to in chapter five. (Do not confuse the initials ICC used here with the Interstate Commerce Commission—this is the International Chamber of Commerce.)

This pamphlet establishes the rules for negotiating a letter of credit. You should have a copy; most international banks provide free copies for their customers.

Conflicting With Publication 500

What about situations in which Publication 500 and the letter of credit conflict?

The driver's license manual says that maximum speed in a residential area is 25 mph, unless posted. So if I am driving down a residential street and there is no sign posted, I can go 25 mph. If I come to a sign that says 15 mph, then that is my speed. If I come to a sign that says 35 mph, then I can speed up.

Likewise, Publication 500 holds true unless otherwise indicated. A letter of credit can stipulate anything an importer directs his or her bank to stipulate, which should, of course, be what the importer and exporter have already agreed to at pro forma stage and earlier, so there are no surprises for the exporter.

Conforming to the Letter of Credit

Suppose something goes wrong under the letter of credit, some minor error. Your bank, the advising bank, would contact the opening bank and ask if the customer still wants the goods despite the error ("wire for approval"). The customer then has the option of authorizing payment or not. Of course, if everything is done exactly in accordance with the letter of credit, you are paid right away and the customer has no chance to change his mind. That is why it is always so important to conform exactly to the letter of credit.

If the customer, decides to deny payment, the documents are returned to you and you still own the merchandise. True, the goods are on board a ship headed for a foreign country, but you still own them and can have them returned or seek another buyer. Of course, if you were paid in advance or were shipping on open account, you could consign the goods directly to the customer.

Truck and rail shipments (say to Canada or Mexico) can be made out to order on special negotiable bills of lading. They would be destined for a particular city with a specific party to notify. (More commonly, they are nonnegotiable and are addressed to the consignee.)

Air shipments are never on a negotiable document. So, on an air letter of credit, it is especially vital to make sure every "i" is dotted and every "t" is crossed.

Naturally, you can always ship direct: Perhaps you have been paid in advance, or you have decided to sell on open account, possibly for a small start-up order.

The words "notify applicant" require that you advise the steamship line of who the actual importer is. Since you are consigning the shipment "to order," you give the importer's name, address and telephone number in a box specifically set aside on the bill of lading for this purpose. I like to type in the words "notify applicant," too. This makes it clear to the bank that yes, this is in fact the applicant listed here.

"Freight prepaid" is a final requirement on the bill of lading. You are in fact paying the freight, so the steamship line will indicate this fact. Since it is a CIF shipment, you expect to pay the freight.

Discrepancies

If you do not conform to the letter of credit exactly you have a *discrepancy*. In this case, the advising bank here advises the opening bank overseas of exactly what the discrepancy is. The opening bank then tells the importer what the discrepancy is and asks if the importer still wants to pay for the goods and accept them.

Remember that if there is any discrepancy whatsoever in your documents, the buyer can change his mind, and you can end up owning the goods ("to order" bills of lading) as they approach the foreign port. On an air shipment, the buyer can change his mind and still pick up the goods. If there are no discrepancies, he cannot change his mind.

Amending the Letter of Credit

What if there is something in the letter of credit that you know is going to result in a discrepancy? Suppose you had agreed with the importer on a specific deadline for shipping and now one of your suppliers is causing delays. You cannot make the deadline that you agreed to in good faith.

The second best thing to do is ask the importer to go to her opening bank and initiate an *amendment* to the letter of credit to change the terms and conditions. The importer's bank sends the amendment to your advising bank, and they send it to you. You decide to accept it or not.

Remember, you do not have to accept an amendment on an irrevocable letter of credit. If the importer extends the shipping time at your request, you will be inclined to accept it. But suppose the amendment states that thirty days extra are granted in exchange for lowering the price 10 percent and wiping out your profit.

The best way to handle the situation is to anticipate it. In spelling everything out at pro forma time allow more time than you feel you need. Ask for ninety days instead of sixty. Assure your buyer that you will ship as quickly as you can (you are anxious to please the buyer and anxious to get paid), but you need the marginal time "just in case."

What, then, if you do not want an amendment, or if you do not want a letter of credit that shows up? Let's say a letter of credit arrives from your bank from someone and it is so completely off base that you cannot honor it. If you do not want it, send it back to the advising bank right away. Either deliver it to the international department and get a receipt, or send it certified mail, return receipt requested. Include a brief letter on your company letterhead stating that you are rejecting the letter of credit. You do not have to give a reason, and you will not be charged.

You should also send a fax to the importer, giving the reasons for rejecting the letter of credit so she can open a new one.

This doesn't happen often. Since a letter of credit can easily be amended by the importer, it is usually better to try to solve the situation through amendment.

I have rejected a letter of credit only once, and that was when the letter of credit was opened by the importer in a third-world country for too brief a period of time. It was mailed from his bank to the U.S. bank and then to us. By the time I received it, the shipping deadline had already passed. So there was no sense playing around with it. I sent it to the bank, certified mail, return receipt requested, and faxed the customer explaining and asking that he start over with a new letter of credit. He didn't. He sent us a check in U.S. funds on a U.S. bank!

Pay Attention to Details

There are three additional points on letters of credit that I caution you not to overlook:

1. Make sure a letter of credit arrives directly from a bank. There is no way a legitimate letter of credit can arrive in your hands directly from the customer. If one ever comes that way, presume it is a forgery and someone is out to cheat you. Take it to your banker.

2. If a letter of credit does arrive from a bank other than yours, you can still ask your bank to be an advising bank on the letter of credit as well. You are putting another layer into the transaction, but now you have a local bank working to check the documents and talk bank-to-bank with the other U.S. bank involved.

Since you requested your bank become involved, you pay the charges of your bank.

3. When a letter of credit arrives from the bank, make a photocopy and go into a room with no phones, by yourself. Take two highlighters in different colors with you, along with a copy of the pro forma invoice.

Go down the copy of the letter of credit line by line. If there is anything that you feel you might have trouble conforming to, or that is in any way different from the pro forma invoice, highlight it in one color to discuss with your associates later. If there is anything you do not quite understand, highlight it in the other color to ask your banker or forwarder later on. The bank will ultimately need the original letter of credit back in order to make payment, so do not make any markings on it.

Letters of Credit and the Importer

As an importer, the letter of credit is exactly the same, except that you are the opener. Your bank will give you an application form in which you will be able to specify all the points listed above.

Be sure to communicate with your exporter (your vendor) prior to opening the letter of credit to be certain that you are opening an letter of credit that is acceptable to you and workable for her.

One paragraph you may want to consider including in your letter of credit application is this:

"Beneficiary must present a certificate that he has

1. sent a fax to the applicant with
   a) name of vessel
   b) sailing date
   c) estimated arrival date and port
   d) bill of lading number, and
2. sent to the applicant by airmail, a copy of each and every document submitted under this letter of credit (photocopies acceptable)."

Because of the time it takes for the documents to come through the banking system, this gives you advance notice of the specifics of the shipment. When the copies arrive, you can give them to your Customs Broker so he can begin work on the shipment even before it arrives.

This goes double for air shipments because they will always beat the documents to your city.

WHICH TERM OF PAYMENT IS BEST?

Possible terms of payment, from the most advantageous for the seller (exporter) to the least advantageous, are:

1. *Prepayment*
2. *Sight letter of credit*
3. *Time letter of credit*
4. *Sight draft*
5. *Time draft*
6. *Open account*

In reverse order, they are from the most advantageous to the buyer (importer) to the least advantageous.

TIME LETTERS OF CREDIT AND TIME DRAFTS

What about *time letters of credit* and *time drafts*? So far, everything we have discussed has been at sight. You are paid right away, either shortly after presentation of the documents under a letter of credit, or shortly after the importer pays his bank under cash against documents. But both letters of credit and drafts can be issued "at thirty days sight," "at ninety days sight," or in any other time frame.

The importer signs the draft, accepting it, and receives his documents. He can claim the goods and clear them through customs, but he has not paid anything. By signing the draft, he is promising to return in thirty days, or ninety days, and pay his bank the money to wire to your bank for your account.

Obviously, in this situation you want to be sure that you can both wait for your money and trust the importer. The difference between this and open account is that the bank in the importer's country now possesses his signature on what amounts to a promissory note, and you can start a lawsuit against him with the note as evidence. If there is a letter of credit, so much the better.

But bear in mind, if the importer is out of business, you can get all the judgments you want and it will not mean anything. Unscrupulous characters roam around in international trade, trying to get their hands on merchandise without paying for it, just as in any sphere of business, anywhere in the world. I caution you against time drafts or time letters of credit unless you are absolutely sure of your customer.

One protection your banker can check into for you is a *banker's acceptance*. Essentially, if the importer defaults, this puts the foreign bank in the importer's place. Now the bank owes you the money at the end of the time frame.

Read about time drafts in the International Chamber of Commerce pamphlet of rules called "Documentary Collections," Publication 322. Be sure to pick it up for your reference library when you visit your international banker.

DIRECT PAYMENT

Of course, the two standard methods of payment in domestic transactions—prepayment and open account—still can be used internationally. But the problems associated with each method of payment (for one party) are more complex than they are with a typical domestic transaction.

Prepayment Considerations

Prepayment is fine from the point of view of the seller. Get paid before you ship. However, as a buyer you can ask yourself "What happens if the seller doesn't ship?"

You could be dealing with an unscrupulous company pocketing the money with no intention of ever shipping the product, or

SIGHT DRAFT AND LETTER OF TRANSMITTAL

U.S. $ 11,075.00   December 14 **19** 95

At Sight _____ of this *FIRST* of Exchange (Second unpaid)

Pay to the Order of Universal Exports

Eleven thousand, seventy-five and 00/100---------------United States Dollars

for Value received and charge the same to account of   Japan Imports

To First Bank of Yokohama

L/C 4129   Universal Exports, by

No. _____   *Joseph Reynolds*
                                                      Authorized Signature

VOID   December 14, 1995
                                                      Date

Gentlemen: ☐ for collection,

We enclose Draft Number L/C 4129 and documents listed below   ☐ for

                                                   ☒ for payment/negotiation under L/C

BILLS OF LADING	B/L COPY	COMM. INV.	INS. CTF.	CTF. ORIG.	CONS. INV.	PKNG. LIST	WGT. CTF.	OTHER DOCUMENTS
3/3	3/3	6/6	2/2	2/2	–	6/6	–	

Please handle in accordance with instructions marked "X"

☐ Deliver all documents in one mailing.

☐ Deliver documents in two mailings.

☐ Deliver documents against payment if sight draft, or acceptance if time draft.

☐ All charges for account of drawee.

☐ Do not waive charges.

☐ Protest for non-payment / non-acceptance

☐ Do not protest.

☐ Present on arrival of goods.

☐ Advise non-payment / non-acceptance by airmail / cable giving reasons.

☐ Advise payment / acceptance by airmail / cable

IN CASE OF NEED refer to:

Name _____

Address _____

who is empowered by us:

a ☐ To act fully on our behalf, i.e., authorize reductions; extensions; free delivery, waiving of protest, etc.

b ☐ To assist in obtaining acceptance or payment of draft, as drawn, but not to alter its terms in any way.

OTHER INSTRUCTIONS:

   Handle in accordance with letter of credit.

Please refer all questions concerning this collection to: Universal Exports by

☒ Shipper (602) 555-1212

☒ Freight Forwarder: (602) 555-9999   *Joseph Reynolds*
   Rio Salado Freight Forwarders   Authorized Signature
   230 North 1 Avenue
   Phoenix, AZ 85025

a seller who goes out of business, or even a seller whose biggest customer goes out of business owing your seller large sums of money, thus forcing your seller out of business. So while prepayment is an ideal method of being paid from the point of view of an exporter, it is risky from the point of view of an importer.

U.S. DOLLARS AT A U.S. BANK

One of the most important things to remember is that you always want to be paid in U.S. dollars at a U.S. bank. This keeps you out of the foreign currency markets and also keeps you from having to wait unduly for a check to clear, payable in U.S. dollars but drawn on a foreign bank.

Your catalogs, pro forma invoices and correspondence should always make this clear:
TERMS:
- *Sight letter of credit in U.S. dollars payable at a U.S. bank.*
- *Check in U.S. dollars payable at a U.S. bank*
- *Wire transfer in U.S. dollars sent to our account at our U.S. bank.*

Open Account Considerations

Under an open account, the seller agrees to ship the goods to the buyer on a net thirty days, net sixty days or other basis (meaning the buyer is to pay in thirty days, sixty days, or whatever the agreed-upon time may be). But what if the buyer sells the goods and doesn't pay? Indeed, what if the principal dies and the family decides to liquidate the business and the money owed you is lost in the shuffle?

Now, this is not to say that prepayment and open account never happen. They can, and they do.

If as an exporter, you receive payment in advance, go ahead and ship. (This is really not uncommon at all when it comes to small transactions and sample shipments, say under USD 500.) If, as an importer, you can convince someone to give you thirty days or sixty days to pay, go ahead and place the order. But either way, the transaction is one-sided and risky to one of the two parties.

Here is a summary of methods of direct payment, whether prepayment or payment being sent when an open account is due.

Paying the Exporter
Wire Transfer

This costs a little money and results in immediate transfer of the money. The buyer (importer) goes to her international bank and directs the bank to send a wire transfer directly to the seller's (exporter's) account in his bank. The money is transferred between the banks overnight, and a deposit slip is mailed to the seller by his bank, showing the deposit of the international funds.

TIP: If you know you will be receiving funds this way, advise your buyer to ask her bank to include this sentence in the covering instructions to your bank:

"Upon Receipt of Funds, Advise Mr. John Q. Seller by telephone, (212) 555-1212."

This way, you will know about the funds the same day they arrive and are available to you, instead of waiting for the deposit slip a day or two later. If you are supposed to ship immediately, this can be of great help.

Check in U.S. Funds on a U.S. Bank

Many international banks overseas maintain checking accounts at U.S. banks and keep the checkbook at their home office in their country. So you might receive a check drawn by the Bank of England on the Bank of California. That type of check will clear as quickly as any check you may receive from a U.S. customer on that California bank.

Cashier's Check or Money Order in U.S. Funds

The cashier's check or money order is drawn by the buyer's bank on their own U.S. dollar account in their own country. The bank has received secure funds from the buyer and issues its own check.

If the check is drawn on an account in a foreign country, however, your U.S. bank may make you wait for the funds until they are received by the U.S. bank. This means you must wait for the document to be sent back to the originating bank and the funds to be sent to the U.S. No matter how secure it is, this method prevents you from having use of your funds as quickly as you would like.

Paying the Importer
Wire Transfer to Foreign Country

When you are importing, your international banker can easily arrange for a wire transfer to the exporter's account in the exporter's home country.

Check in Foreign Funds on a Foreign Bank

Most of the larger U.S. banks handling international transactions maintain checking accounts in foreign funds in banks all over the world. So you can have checks drawn in deutschemarks, pounds sterling, French or Swiss francs, etc., and the checks are payable at banks in the country of the currency. You are handed the check and send it to the exporter yourself.

Cashier's Check or Money Order in U.S. Dollars

Your bank will be glad to sell you either a cashier's check or a money order. In fact,

you can obtain an international money order at any U.S. post office. But, despite the secure funds, when the check is deposited in the seller's account in a foreign bank, the bank normally makes the seller wait for the funds until they are received through the banking system as outlined above.

So, while prepayments and open accounts are feasible, there is some risk and a certain amount of awkwardness involved in their use.

CASH AGAINST DOCUMENTS

There is one final way to arrange payment, and that is called *cash against documents*—a "letter of credit without a letter of credit." You already know how to do one. Take the example transaction from Universal Exports to Japan Imports. Remove the letter of credit.

Have the documents issued just as before, with original bills of lading and insurance issued "to order." All the documents go to your international bank in your city with instructions to send all the documents to the bank of your importer in Tokyo. Upon arrival of the documents, the importer's bank calls him and asks him to sign the draft and turn over USD 14,200 plus banking fees.

After he signs the draft and presents the funds, the importer receives the documents and can pick up the shipment and arrange customs clearance.

"Ah," you say. "But he can also change his mind. He can refuse to accept the documents."

Go to the head of the class!

With a sight draft, you do not have the protection of a letter of credit, but it is also a step removed from open account. If the importer refuses to pay, he doesn't get the merchandise either. You still own the goods, or you are stuck with them in a foreign port. It all depends on your point of view.

Obviously, this procedure works best with a customer you have a good deal of faith in but are not quite ready to trust with open account shipments.

You can read more about cash against documents in the ICC Publication 322, the same pamphlet that details rules for time drafts.

Documentation

- *The Commercial Invoice*
- *The Packing Slip*
- *The Bill of Lading*
- *Shipper's Export Declaration*
- *Certificate of Origin*
- *Legalization and Consularization*
- *Canada Customs Invoice*
- *NAFTA Certificate of Origin*
- *Export Vessel Movement Summary Sheet*
- *Postal Service Forms*
- *Insurance Policy*

If you're an exporter, you need not worry much about documentation because: (1) your customer will tell you what documents he needs; and (2) your forwarder can prepare any of the documents for you if you prefer not to do them yourself. It is good to know what documents are involved, of course.

As an importer, the situation is a little different. You not only need the documents required by U.S. Customs, but also the documents that might be required by any other federal, state or local agency regulating your commodity.

In this chapter I'll discuss types of documentation that are part and parcel of international trade. Keep in mind that if you need help, you have an expert on documentation at the other end of your telephone—your freight forwarder. Your forwarder will be glad to do any or all of the documents for you for a small fee. Remember, if you're not 100 percent certain, the cheapest route is to retain expert assistance.

THE COMMERCIAL INVOICE

If you are an exporter, the commercial invoice is one of the two easiest documents you'll use. It is the same invoice you use now to bill your customers. Of course, it must be issued in accordance with the requirements under the letter of credit. The sample on page 71 is a typical commercial invoice for an export transaction.

There are two special requirements for export. First, you must show the terms of sale: FOB, CIF, etc. Second, you must identify the country where the goods actually originated. If they were manufactured in the United States, type the following statement on the invoice:

"This is to certify that these goods were manufactured in the United States of America and that this is a true and correct invoice."

Type your company name next and sign the statement. This signed statement will assist your customer in Customs clearance at the other end.

FORMS

Some forms, such as NAFTA Certificates of Origin, follow specific formats. You can purchase the forms or have your freight forwarder prepare them.

Two forms that do not have to be in a specific format are:

1. Commercial invoice
2. Packing slip

The commercial invoice needs to have the pricing and the packing slip needs to show how the goods are packed, but as to format, you can use your regular invoice and packing slip, your letterhead, or a plain piece of paper. Preprinted generic forms are also available at stationery stores. The type of information required is shown on page 71.

THE PACKING SLIP

The packing slip (also called *packing list*) is easy—you use it now. Refer to the sample on page 71. The format is the same as for an invoice except that it does not show the prices and it shows how the goods are packed. This sample shows ten cartons of one hundred books per carton, numbered 1 through 10.

THE BILL OF LADING

There are three types of bills of lading: ocean bills of lading, truck bills of lading and air waybills.

Ocean Bills of Lading

Normally, the freight forwarder prepares a set of bills of lading that are sent by mail or messenger to the steamship line. After sailing, the steamship line processes the

SAMPLE COMMERCIAL INVOICE

FROM: Universal Exports   Invoice 8124
       1700 West Washington Street
       Phoenix, AZ 85007 U.S.A.

TO: Japan Imports
       147 Chuo-Ku
       Yokohama, Japan

DATE: December 15, 1995

1,000 (one thousand) copies of International Business, @ USD 10.00

CIF Yokohama (Cost, Insurance, and Freight)   USD 14,200.00

Export Packing Included

This is to certify that these goods were manufactured in the United States of America and that this is a true and correct invoice.

Universal Exports by *Joseph Reynolds*

SAMPLE PACKING SLIP

FROM: Universal Exports   Invoice 8124
       1700 West Washington Street
       Phoenix, AZ 85007 U.S.A.

TO: Japan Imports
       147 Chuo-Ku
       Yokohama, Japan

DATE: December 15, 1995

10 cartons
numbered 1/10
containing: 1,000 (one thousand) copies of International Business

1,000 lbs (454 Kgs.)
37.50 cubic feet (1.09 M3)

Shipment: Via Vessel

bills, indicating the sailing date and other information.

Three of the bills are stamped "On Board" and are signed by or on behalf of the captain. If they are made out "to order of shipper," as in the example (see page 73), in accordance with the letter of credit, they then constitute the actual title to the goods as far as the steamship line is concerned. (I discussed this in detail in chapter seven.) The other copies are stamped "Copy, Not Negotiable," and these copies are distributed to everyone involved with the shipment, including file copies for you.

Of course, a shipment for which you have already been paid can be sent directly consigned to the importer.

The steamship line rates the bills of lading and returns them to your forwarder for distribution. You will receive your nonnegotiable file copies.

Truck Bills of Lading

If you have an inland shipment to Canada or Mexico, you normally prepare only a truck bill of lading. The two kinds of truck bills of lading are: nonnegotiable and negotiable.

Nonnegotiable

Nonnegotiable bills of lading are the most common and direct the trucker to ship your goods to the consignee (addressee) and deliver them. These are white. (See page 74.)

Negotiable

The original of a negotiable bill of lading (page 75) is yellow and, like an ocean bill of lading issued to order, constitutes title to the goods.

Air Waybill

The air waybill (page 76) is never negotiable. When you send a shipment by air, it is always consigned directly to a particular company or person.

Air Couriers

You can ship via companies such as DHL, Federal Express and UPS. However, their waybills are not negotiable either and must be addressed to a specific consignee. So, as with any air waybill, be very careful of discrepancies in the letter of credit.

SHIPPER'S EXPORT DECLARATION

The shipper's export declaration is a form required in duplicate by the United States government for all export shipments unless (1) they are valued at $2,499.99 or less, or (2) they are shipments with Canada as the ultimate destination. In either case the shipment does not require a validated export license as discussed in chapter one. The form is not very complicated. Most of the information is information you already put on commercial invoices: your name and address, consignee's name and address, etc.

Here is a discussion of the new information. See page 77 for a sample of the form.

Field 1b, Exporter EIN (IRS) No.: Your EIN number is your IRS Employer Identification Number or, if you are exporting as an individual, your Social Security Number.

Field 1c, Parties to Transaction: The "parties" (the exporter and the importer) are related if they are naturally related (individuals who are relatives) or companies under common control (subsidiaries or branches trading with each other). Otherwise, they are not related.

Fields 4a and 4b, Ultimate Consignee; Intermediate Consignee: The ultimate consignee is the company or person actually receiving the goods. You may or may not have an intermediate consignee between you and the ultimate consignee. For

OCEAN BILL OF LADING

SEA-LAND SERVICE, INC.

INTERNATIONAL BILL OF LADING
NOT NEGOTIABLE UNLESS CONSIGNED "TO ORDER"
(SPACES IMMEDIATELY BELOW FOR SHIPPERS' MEMORANDA)

(2) SHIPPER/EXPORTER (COMPLETE NAME AND ADDRESS) Universal Exports 1700 West Washington Street Phoenix, AZ 85007	(5) BOOKING NO. LAX456YOK / (5A) BILL OF LADING NO. 1245621
	(6) EXPORT REFERENCES Invoice 8124
(3) CONSIGNEE (COMPLETE NAME AND ADDRESS) To Order of Shipper	(7) FORWARDING AGENT/F M C NO. Rio Salado Freight Forwarders FMC 9999 230 North 1 Avenue Phoenix, AZ 85025
	(8) POINT AND COUNTRY OF ORIGIN Arizona, U.S.A.
(4) NOTIFY PARTY (COMPLETE NAME AND ADDRESS) Japan Imports 147 Chuo-Ku Yokohama, Japan	(9) ALSO NOTIFY - ROUTING & INSTRUCTIONS Trans-Port Express to Pier

(12) INITIAL CARRIAGE BY (MODE) * truck	(13) PLACE OF INITIAL RECEIPT * Pier G, Berth 228	(9A) FINAL DESTINATION (OF THE GOODS NOT THE SHIP) Yokohama, Japan	
(14) VESSEL VOY FLAG Explorer, 12W U.S.	(15) PORT OF LOADING Long Beach, CA	(10) LOADING PIER/TERMINAL Pier G, Berth 228	(10A) ORIGINAL(S) TO BE RELEASED AT Long Beach, CA
(16) PORT OF DISCHARGE Yokohama	(17) PLACE OF DELIVERY BY ON-CARRIER * --	(11) TYPE OF MOVE (IF MIXED, USE BLOCK 20 AS APPROPRIATE) ocean	

PARTICULARS FURNISHED BY SHIPPER

MKS. & NOS./CONT. NOS. (18)	NO. OF PKGS. (19)	HM**	DESCRIPTION OF PACKAGES AND GOODS (20)	GROSS WEIGHT (21)	MEASUREMENT (22)
As Addresses 1/10 (LCL) VOID	10		textbooks NON-NEGOTIABLE OCEAN FREIGHT PREPAID	455 Kgs	1.09 M3

(23) DECLARED VALUE $	IF SHIPPER ENTERS A VALUE, CARRIERS "PACKAGE" LIMITATIONS OF LIABILITY DOES NOT APPLY AND THE AD VALOREM RATE WILL BE CHARGED.	(24) FREIGHT PAYABLE AT/BY Long Beach, CA b

FREIGHT CHARGES	RATED AS	PER	RATE	PREPAID	COLLECT	CURRENCY/RATE OF EXCHANGE
Ocean Freight	1.09	M3	261.00	284.49		USD
CAF	39%		110.95	110.95		USD
Fuel Adj.	1.09	M3	3.00	3.27		USD
Origin Receiv.	1.09	M3	29.00	31.61		USD
Dest. Delivery	1.09	M3	3680.00		4011.20	¥

THE RECEIPT, CUSTODY, CARRIAGE AND DELIVERY OF THE GOODS ARE SUBJECT TO THE TERMS APPEARING ON THE FACE AND BACK HEREOF AND TO CARRIER'S APPLICABLE TARIFF.

TOTALS ▶   430.32   4011.20

In witness whereof   **3**   original bills of lading all the same tenor and date one of which being accomplished the others to stand void, have been issued by Sea-Land Service. Inc. or its designated agent on behalf of itself, other participating carriers, the vessel, her master and owners or charterers.

* APPLICABLE ONLY WHEN USED FOR MULTIMODAL OR THROUGH TRANSPORTATION
** INDICATE WHETHER ANY OF THE CARGO IS HAZARDOUS MATERIAL UNDER DOT, IMCO OR OTHER REGULATIONS AND INDICATE CORRECT COMMODITY NUMBER IN BOX 20.

AT Long Beach, California, U.S.A.

BY ....
FOR SEA-LAND SERVICE, INC.

SL-2855 (1/94)   BILL OF LADING NO.   DATE

TRUCK BILL OF LADING—NOT NEGOTIABLE

STRAIGHT BILL OF LADING—SHORT FORM—ORIGINAL—NOT NEGOTIABLE

RECEIVED, subject to the classifications and tariffs in effect on the date of the issue of this Bill of Lading, the property described above in apparent good order, except as noted (contents and condition of contents of packages unknown), marked, consigned, and destined as indicated above which said carrier (the word carrier being understood throughout this contract as meaning any person or corporation in possession of the property under the contract) agrees to carry to its usual place of delivery at said destination, if on its route, otherwise to deliver to another carrier on the route to said destination. It is mutually agreed as to each carrier

of all or any of said property over all or any portion of said route to destination and as to each party at any time interested in all or any said property, that every service to be performed hereunder shall be subject to all the bill of lading terms and conditions in the governing classification on the date of shipment.

Shipper hereby certifies that he is familiar with all the bill of lading terms and conditions in the governing classification and the said terms and conditions are hereby agreed to by the shipper and accepted for himself and his assigns.

From ___Universal Exports___

At ___Phoenix, AZ___   ___Dec 4___ 19_95_ BY TRUCK ☒ FREIGHT ☐ Shipper's No. ___8124___

DESIGNATE WITH AN (X)

Carrier ___Trans-Port Express___   Agent's No. _____

(Mail or street address of consignee—For purposes of notification only.)

Consigned to ___Sea-Land Explorer, Voyage 12W, Booking Number LAX456YOK___

Destination ___Pier G, Berth 228, Long Beach___   State of ___CA 90801___   County of _____

Route___Trans-Port Express to destination___

Delivering Carrier ___Trans-Port Express___   Vehicle or Car Initial _____   No. _____

No. Packages	Kind of Package, Description of Articles, Special Marks, and Exceptions	*Weight (Sub. to Cor.)	Class or Rate	Check Column	
10	cartons textbooks, NMFC 161560	1,000	65		Subject to Section 7 of conditions of applicable bill of lading, if this shipment is to be delivered to the consignee without recourse on the consignor, the consignor shall sign the following statement: The carrier shall not make delivery of this shipment without payment of freight and all other lawful charges.
					Per _____ (Signature of Consignor.)
					If charges are to be prepaid, write or stamp here, "To be Prepaid."
	FOR EXPORT TO ULTIMATE DESTINATION:				TO BE PREPAID
	YOKOHAMA, JAPAN				Received $ _____ to apply in prepayment of the charges on the property described hereon.
	FORWARDER:				_____ Agent or Cashier
	RIO SALADO FREIGHT FORWARDERS				Per _____ (The signature here acknowledges only the amount prepaid.)
					Charges Advanced:
	VOID				**C.O.D. SHIPMENT** Prepaid ☐ Collect ☐ $_____ Collection Fee _____ Total Charges _____
					*If the shipment moves between two ports by a carrier by water, the law requires that the bill of lading shall state whether it is "Carrier's or Shipper's weight."
					†Shipper's imprint in lieu of stamp; not a part of bill of lading approved by the Department of Transportation.
					NOTE—Where the rate is dependent on value, shippers are required to state specifically in writing the agreed or declared value of the property.
					THIS SHIPMENT IS CORRECTLY DESCRIBED. CORRECT WEIGHT IS _____ LBS.
					Subject to verification by the Respective Weighing and Inspection Bureau According to Agreement. Per _____

TOTAL PIECES |

† "The fibre containers used for this shipment conform to the specifications set forth in the box maker's certificate thereon, and all other requirements of Rule 41 of the Uniform Freight Classification and Rule 5 of the National Motor Freight Classification." † Shipper's imprint in lieu of stamp, not a part of bill of lading approved by Interstate Commerce Commission.

If lower charges result, the agreed or declared value of the within described containers is hereby specifically stated by the shipper to be not exceeding 50 cents per pound per article.

___Universal Exports___   _Joseph Reynolds_ Shipper, Per

___Trans-Port Express___   Agent, Per _M. Bond_

This is to certify that the above-named materials are properly classified, described, packaged, marked and labeled and are in proper condition for transportation according to the applicable regulations of the Department of Transportation.

Permanent post-office address of shipper
___1700 West Washington Street, Phoenix, AZ 85007___

1

_____ SIGNATURE

TRUCK BILL OF LADING—NEGOTIABLE

RULES

(To be Printed on "Yellow" Paper)

UNIFORM ORDER BILL OF LADING

Original—Domestic

Shipper's No. 9144
Agent's No.

Trans-Port Express

Carrier_____ (SCAC)

RECEIVED, subject to the classifications and lawfully filed tariffs in effect on the date of the issue of this Bill of Lading.

From Universal Exports   Date January 11 19 96

At 1700 Street W. Washington City Phoenix County _____ State AZ zip 85007

the property described below, in apparent good order, except as noted (contents and condition of contents of packages unknown) marked, consigned, and destined as shown below, which said company (the word company being understood throughout this contract as meaning any person or corporation in possession of the property under the contract) agrees to carry to its usual place of delivery at said destination, if on its own railroad, water line, highway route or routes, or within the territory of its highway operations, otherwise to deliver to another carrier on the route to said destination. It is mutually agreed, as to each carrier of all or any of said property over all or any portion of said route to destination, and as to each party at any time interested in all or any of said property, that every service to be performed hereunder shall be subject to all the conditions not prohibited by law, whether printed or written, herein contained, including the conditions on the back hereof, which are hereby agreed to by the shipper and accepted for himself and his assigns.

The surrender of this Original ORDER Bill of Lading properly indorsed shall be required before the delivery of the property. Inspection of property conveyed by this bill of lading will not be permitted unless provided by law or unless permission is indorsed on this original bill of lading or given in writing by the shipper.

Consigned to Order of shipper

Destination _____ Street _____ City Nogales County _____ State AZ zip 85621

Notify Rio Salado Customs Brokers

At Terrace @ Intl. Street _____ City Nogales County _____ State AZ zip 85621

Routing Trans-Port Express

Delivering Carrier Trans-Port Express Vehicle or Car Initial _____ No. _____

No. Pack-ages	✪ HM	Kind of Package, Description of Articles, Special Marks, and Exceptions	*Weight (Subject to Correction)	Class or Rate	Check Column	
10		cartons textbooks				Subject to Section 7 of conditions, if the shipment is to be delivered to the consignee without recourse on the consignor, the consignor shall sign the following statement:
		NMFC 161560	1,000	65		The carrier shall not make delivery of this shipment without payment of freight and all other lawful charges.
						_____
						(Signature of consignor)
			VOID			
						If charges are to be prepaid write or stamp here "To be Prepaid."
		ULTIMATE DESTINATION:				TO BE PREPAID
		MEXICO IMPORTS,				
		MEXICO CITY, MEXICO				Received $ _____ to apply in prepayment of the charges on the property described hereon.
						Agent or Cashier
						Per _____ (The signature here acknowledges only the amount prepaid)

*If the shipment moves between two ports by a carrier by water, the law requires that the bill of lading shall state whether it is "carrier's or shipper's weight."

NOTE—(1) Where the rate is dependent on value, shippers are required to state specifically in writing the agreed or declared value of the property, as follows:

"The agreed or declared value of the property is hereby specifically stated by the shipper to be not exceeding _____ per _____."

Ⓥ (2) Where the applicable tariff provisions specify a limitation of the carrier's liability absent a release or a value declaration by the shipper and the shipper does not release the carrier's liability or declare a value, the carrier's liability shall be limited to the extent provided by such provisions. See NMFC Item 172.

Charges advanced:

$ _____

Universal Exports   Shipper   Trans-Port Express   Agent

Per *Joseph Reynolds*   Per *N. Bond*

Permanent address of Shipper: Street 1700 W. Washington City Phoenix State AZ Zip 85007

✪ Mark with "X" to designate Hazardous Materials as defined in the Department of Transportation Regulations governing the transportation of hazardous materials. The use of this column is an optional method for identifying hazardous materials on bills of lading per Section 172.201(a)(1)(iii) of Title 49, Code of Federal Regulations. Also, when shipping hazardous materials, the shipper's certification statement prescribed in Section 172.204(a) of the Federal Regulations must be indicated on the bill of lading, unless a specific exception from this requirement is provided in the Regulations for a particular material.

Ⓥ - This paragraph does not apply on California intrastate traffic.

AIR WAYBILL

		House Air Waybill Number

Shipper's Name and Address   **Shipper's account Number**

Universal Exports
1700 West Washington Street
Phoenix, AZ 85007 U.S.A.

12345

Not negotiable
Air Waybill
(Air Consignment note)
Issued by

     XYZ Airlines

Copies 1, 2 and 3 of this Air Waybill are originals and have the same validity.

Consignee's Name and Address   **Consignee's account Number**

Japan Imports
147 Chuo-ku
Yokohama, Japan
c/o Japan Brokers, Tokyo Airport

It is agreed that the goods described herein are accepted in apparent good order and condition (except as noted) for carriage SUBJECT TO THE CONDITIONS OF CONTRACT ON THE REVERSE HEREOF. THE SHIPPER'S ATTENTION IS DRAWN TO THE NOTICE CONCERNING CARRIERS' LIMITATION OF LIABILITY. Shipper may increase such limitation of liability by declaring a higher value for carriage and paying a supplemental charge if required.

These commodities licensed by the United States for ultimate destination

     Japan   Diversion contrary to

United States law prohibited.

VOID

Airport of Departure (Addr. of first Carrier) and requested Routing

Phoenix, XYZ to destination

to	By first Carrier / Routing and Destination / Air Waybill Number	Currency	CHGS Code	WT/VAL PPD COLL	Other PPD COLL	Declared Value for Carriage	Declared Value for Customs
TYO	XYZ	USD	X			11,500.00	10,150.00

Airport of Destination   Flight/Date   For Carrier Use only   Flight/Date   **Amount of Insurance**

Yokohama   12,182.50

INSURANCE: If Carrier offers insurance and such insurance is requested in accordance with conditions on reverse hereof, indicate amount to be insured in figures in box marked "amount of insurance".

Handling Information

No. of Pieces RCP	Gross Weight	kg lb	Rate Class / Commodity Item No.	Chargeable Weight	Rate / Charge	Total	Nature and Quantity of Goods (incl. Dimensions or Volume)
10	455	K	G 213a	455	3.50/Kg	1592.50	textbooks 1.09M3
10	455					1592.50	

Prepaid	Weight Charge	**Collect**	Other Charges
1592.50			Forwarding + Insurance, $75.25, Cartage, $35.00

	Valuation Charge	

	Tax	

	Total other Charges Due Agent	
110.25		

	Total other Charges Due Carrier	

Shipper certifies that the particulars on the face hereof are correct and that insofar as any part of the consignment contains dangerous goods such part is properly described by name and is in proper condition for carriage by air according to the applicable Dangerous Goods Regulations.

Joseph Reynolds

Signature of Shipper or his Agent

Total prepaid	Total collect
1702.75	

Currency Conversion Rates	cc charges in Dest. Currency

December 14, 1995   Phoenix   *Al Sanders*

Executed on   (Date)   at   (Place)   Signature of Issuing Carrier or its Agent

House Air Waybill Number

SHIPPER'S EXPORT DECLARATION

U.S. DEPARTMENT OF COMMERCE—BUREAU OF THE CENSUS—INTERNATIONAL TRADE ADMINISTRATION

FORM **7525-V** (1-1-88)   **SHIPPER'S EXPORT DECLARATION**   OMB No. 0607-0018

1a. EXPORTER (Name and address including ZIP code)
Universal Exports
1700 West Washington Street
Phoenix, AZ

ZIP CODE
85007

2. DATE OF EXPORTATION
December 14, 1995

3. BILL OF LADING/AIR WAYBILL NO.
1245621

b. EXPORTER EIN (IRS) NO.
55-1234567

c. PARTIES TO TRANSACTION
☐ Related   ☒ Non-related

4a. ULTIMATE CONSIGNEE
Japan Imports
147 Chuo-ku, Yokohama, Japan

b. INTERMEDIATE CONSIGNEE
none

5. FORWARDING AGENT
Rio Salado Freight Forwarders FMC 9999
230 North 1 Avenue
Phoenix, AZ 85025

6. POINT (STATE) OF ORIGIN OR FTZ NO.
AZ

7. COUNTRY OF ULTIMATE DESTINATION
Japan

8. LOADING PIER (Vessel only)
Pier G, Berth 228

9. MODE OF TRANSPORT (Specify)
vessel

10. EXPORTING CARRIER
Explorer

11. PORT OF EXPORT
Long Beach, CA

12. PORT OF UNLOADING (Vessel and air only)
Yokohama

13. CONTAINERIZED (Vessel only)
☒ Yes   ☐ No

VOID

14. SCHEDULE B DESCRIPTION OF COMMODITIES,
15. MARKS, NOS., AND KINDS OF PACKAGES } (Use columns 17-19)

D/F (16)	SCHEDULE B NUMBER (17)	CHECK DIGIT	QUANTITY—SCHEDULE B UNIT(S) (18)	SHIPPING WEIGHT (Kilos) (19)	VALUE (U.S. dollars, omit cents) (Selling price or cost if not sold) (20)
D	As Addressed, 10 cartons textbooks 4901.99.0010	2	1,000	455	10,150.

THESE COMMODITIES LICENSED BY THE UNITED STATES
FOR ULTIMATE DESTINATION JAPAN. DIVERSION CONTRARY
TO UNITED STATES LAW PROHIBITED.

21. VALIDATED LICENSE NO./GENERAL LICENSE SYMBOL
G-DEST

22. ECCN (When required)
N/A

23. Duly authorized officer or employee
Joseph Reynolds

The exporter authorizes the forwarder named above to act as forwarding agent for export control and customs purposes.

24. I certify that all statements made and all information contained herein are true and correct and that I have read and understand the instructions for preparation of this document, set forth in the "Correct Way to Fill Out the Shipper's Export Declaration" (available Bureau of Census, Wash., DC 20233). I understand that civil and criminal penalties, including forfeiture and sale, may be imposed for making false or fraudulent statements herein, failing to provide the requested information or for violation of U.S. laws on exportation (13 U.S.C. Sec. 305; 22 U.S.C. Sec. 401; 18 U.S.C. Sec. 1001; 50 U.S.C. App. 2410).

Signature *Joseph Reynolds*

Confidential—For use solely for official purposes authorized by the Secretary of Commerce (13 U.S.C. 301 (g)).

Title Export Manager

Export shipments are subject to inspection by U.S. Customs Service and/or Office of Export Enforcement.

Date Dec. 14, 1995

25. AUTHENTICATION (When required)
N/A

example, you may be selling a computer to ABC Data Processing Company in London, but you may be first shipping it to XYZ Computer Company to test it and set it up on site.

Field 6, Point (State) of Origin or FTZ No.: This is the U.S. state from which the export shipment originates. Normally, that is your state. FTZ means foreign trade zone, and you will learn about those in chapter twelve. You probably will not be using one when you first start out.

Fields 9-13, Mode of Transport; Exporting Carrier; Port of Export; Port of Unloading; Containerized: This is shipment information that your forwarder can supply to you. Or, if you wish, you can let your forwarder complete the form.

Field 14, Schedule B Description of Commodities: The Schedule B Description of Commodities is found in the *Harmonized System Schedule B* book available through the Department of Commerce or in many public libraries (see sample on page 80). All goods can be classified by Schedule B number and must be classified on the export declaration.

All forwarders have copies of the Schedule B, so you don't need to buy one, and your forwarder can find the classifications for your goods. You will probably specialize in certain commodities and will only need a handful of Schedule B numbers no matter how long you are in the export business.

In this example, copies of *International Business* qualify as textbooks. Where it says "Use columns 17-19," this simply means that you can type this information across those three columns.

Field 15, Marks, Nos., and Kinds of Packages: In this case, the cartons are marked "as addressed," to your customer; are numbered 1 through 10; and are cartons rather than drums or crates.

Field 16, D/F: If the product was manufactured in the United States, indicate "D" for domestic. If it was manufactured outside the United States and is now being reexported, mark "F" for foreign.

Field 17, Schedule B Number: This is the Schedule B number from the Schedule B book. The last digit of the eleven-digit number goes in the Check Digit column.

Field 18, Quantity—Schedule B Unit(s): For textbooks, you are required to list the quantity in terms of the number of textbooks. Some commodities may need to be listed by weight or other measurement. If an "X" appears on the Schedule B, no quantity is indicated—just put down X.

Field 20, Value: This is the FAS price if you are selling the goods. (Even if you are selling FCA or CIF, you compute the price for this column as if it were sold FAS. This keeps all statistics consistent.)

If you are not selling the product (perhaps you are shipping some advertising material at no charge), you base the value on your cost plus shipping to the port of export, to arrive at an FAS price.

Along the bottom of the main block, type the "diversion clause" as shown, naming the country of ultimate destination.

Field 21, Validated License No./General License Symbol: If you are shipping goods under a validated license from the U.S. government (e.g., to sell high-tech computers to Mexico, license number A123456), put this information here. If you are shipping goods that do not require a validated license, a general license designation applies. Usually, you would indicate G-DEST for general license to the destination. Other abbreviations are used from time to time, and your forwarder will be glad to help you here.

Field 22, ECCN: ECCN stands for Export Commodity Control Numbers. These are needed only for exports that require validated licenses. You may never even have one. If you do, you will obtain this number from the Department of Commerce in the process of applying for the license.

Field 23: Sign here to authorize the forwarder to handle the shipment for you. This is basically just a very brief power of attorney.

Field 24: Sign here to certify that you are telling the truth.

If you are at all concerned about properly completing the export declaration, rest easy: I guarantee your forwarder does them by the hundreds and will be glad to do yours. If you do want to do your own, or just want to find out more, call or visit your local office of the U.S. Department of Commerce's U.S. and Foreign Commercial Service. Ask for your free copy of "Correct Way to Fill Out the Shipper's Export Declarations," booklet 7525-V(INST).

Here's a tip: If you call the export declaration an ex dec with forwarders, you will sound as though you have been exporting for years.

All forwarders will supply you with Shipper's Letter of Instructions (see page 81) forms free. These have an instructional form for the forwarder on top, and copies of the yellow export declaration below. Parts that you leave blank are completed by the forwarder.

CERTIFICATE OF ORIGIN

A certificate of origin is sometimes requested by an importer overseas. This is usually a generic form readily available from supply houses that specialize in international documents (see the Resource List at the back of the book for a listing of these supply houses). As you can see, it follows the format for the ocean bill of lading.

Some importers only want you to supply a certificate with your signature at the bottom. Others ask that you have your signature notarized. Still others ask that it be notarized and also approved by your local chamber of commerce. Your chamber of commerce will approve your certificates of origin based on your notarized statement that the goods originated in the United States. They usually charge a small fee, but you generally do not have to be a chamber of commerce member.

Sometimes you must supply a special certificate of origin. For example, the United States has a Free Trade Agreement with Israel that requires a special certificate of origin.

See pages 82 and 83 for some examples of certificates of origin.

LEGALIZATION AND CONSULARIZATION

Some countries require that some of the documents be sent to their consulate in the United States for approval. This is called *legalization* or consularization. Your forwarder will be very familiar with this process.

Usually, the invoice and certificate of origin, and possibly the packing slip, need to be legalized. Sometimes the bill of lading or other documents are included.

Normally, the importer's broker advises him that a shipment requires legalization, and he inserts that requirement in the letter of credit. Documents presented without legalization will not be accepted by the bank.

Legalization is most common for Middle East countries (other than Israel), Latin America, Africa, and some of the smaller countries of Asia. This is a lot of territory, but the United States' major trading partners (Europe, Australia and New Zealand, and Japan) don't require legalization, so you may never run into it.

If legalization is needed and the shipment is FOB or farther along, you must be

SCHEDULE B

Classification of Exports

Sched. B No. and Headings	Chk Dgt	Commodity Description	Unit of Quantity
4901		Printed books, brochures, leaflets and similar printed matter, whether or not in single sheets:	
4901.10.0000	0	In single sheets, whether or not folded............	X
		Other:	
4901.91		Dictionaries and encyclopedias, and serial installments thereof:	
4901.91.0020	8	Dictionaries including thesauruses...........	No.
4901.91.0040	4	Encyclopedias and serial installments thereof.	No.
4901.99		Other:	
4901.99.0010	2	Textbooks.................................	No.
4901.99.0020	0	Bound newspapers, journals and periodicals provided for in note 3 of this chapter.......	No.
4901.99.0030	8	Directories...............................	No.
		Other:	
4901.99.0040	6	Bibles, testaments, prayer books and other religious books...........................	No.
4901.99.0050	3	Technical, scientific and professional books..................................	No.
4901.99.0055	8	Art and pictorial books...................	No.
		Other:	
4901.99.0070	9	Hardbound books.......................	No.
4901.99.0075	4	Rack size paperbound books	No.
4901.99.0090	5	Other.................................	No.
4902		Newspapers, journals and periodicals, whether or not illustrated or containing advertising material:	
4902.10.0000	9	Appearing at least four times a week...............	kg
4902.90		Other:	
4902.90.2020	4	Newspapers appearing less than four times a week.	kg
4902.90.2040	0	Other business and professional journals and periodicals (including single issues tied together for shipping purposes).................	No.
4902.90.5000	1	Other (including single issues tied together for shipping purposes)............................	No.
4903.00.0000	0	Children's picture, drawing or coloring books	X

SHIPPER'S LETTER OF INSTRUCTIONS

SHIPPER (Name and address including ZIP code) Universal Exports 1700 West Washington Street Phoenix, AZ	ZIP CODE 85007	INLAND CARRIER (See note #2 below)	SHIP DATE	PRO NO.

EXPORTER EIN (IRS) NO. 55-1234567	PARTIES TO TRANSACTION ☐ Related ☒ Non-related	

ULTIMATE CONSIGNEE
Japan Imports
147 Chuo-ku, Yokohama, Japan

INTERMEDIATE CONSIGNEE
None

FORWARDING AGENT
Rio Salado Freight Forwarders FMC 9999
230 North 1 Avenue
Phoenix, AZ 85025

POINT (STATE) OF ORIGIN OR FTZ NO. AZ	COUNTRY OF ULTIMATE DESTINATION Japan

SHIPPER'S LETTER OF INSTRUCTIONS

NOTE:
① IF YOU ARE UNCERTAIN OF THE SCHEDULE B COMMODITY NO.—DO NOT TYPE IT IN—WE WILL COMPLETE WHEN PROCESSING THE 7525-V.
② IF YOU HAVE SHIPPED THIS MATERIAL TO US VIA AN INLAND CARRIER—PLEASE GIVE US THE INLAND CARRIER'S NAME, SHIPPING DATE, AND RECEIPT OR PRO. NO. (IF AVAILABLE). THIS WILL HELP US EXPEDITE YOUR SHIPMENT WITH THE INLAND CARRIER.
③ BE SURE TO PICK UP TOP SHEET AND SIGN THE FIRST BUFF EXPORT DECLARATION WITH PEN AND INK.

SHIPPER'S REF. NO. 8124	DATE Dec. 10, 1995	SHIP VIA ☐ AIR ☒ OCEAN	☐ CONSOLIDATE	☐ DIRECT

	SCHEDULE B DESCRIPTION OF COMMODITIES					VALUE (U.S. dollars, omit cents) (Selling price or cost if not sold)
D/F	MARKS, NOS., AND KIND OF PKGS. SCHEDULE B NUMBER	QUANTITY— SCHEDULE B UNIT(S)	SHIPPING WEIGHT (Kilos)	SHIPPING WEIGHT (Pounds)	CUBIC METERS	
D	As Addressed, 10 cartons textbooks		455	1,000	1.09	10,150.

VOID

VALIDATED LICENSE NO./GENERAL LICENSE SYMBOL G-DEST	ECCN (When required) N/A	SHIPPER MUST CHECK ♦ ☒ PREPAID OR ☐ COLLECT

Duly authorized officer or employee
Joseph Reynolds

The exporter authorizes the forwarder named above to act as forwarding agent for export control and customs purposes.

C.O.D. AMOUNT $

SPECIAL INSTRUCTIONS

Handle in accordance with letter of credit.

BE SURE TO PICK UP TOP SHEET AND SIGN THE FIRST BUFF EXPORT DECLARATION WITH PEN & INK.

SHIPPER'S INSTRUCTIONS IN CASE OF INABILITY TO DELIVER
CONSIGNMENT AS CONSIGNED: ☐ ABANDON ☐ RETURN TO SHIPPER
☐ DELIVER TO _____ Advise shipper

SHIPPER'S REQUESTS INSURANCE	☐ NO ☒ YES $12182.50	If Shipper has requested insurance as provided for at the left hereof, shipment is insured in the amount indicated (recovery is limited to actual loss) in accordance with the provisions as specified in the Carrier's Tariffs. Insurance is payable to Shipper unless payee is designated in writing by the shipper.

NOTE: The Shipper or his Authorized Agent hereby authorizes the above named Company, in his name and on his behalf, to prepare any export documents, to sign and accept any documents relating to said shipment and forward this shipment in accordance with the conditions of carriage and the tariffs of the carriers employed. The shipper guarantees payment of all collect charges in the event the consignee refuses payment. Hereunder the sole responsibility of the Company is to use reasonable care in the selection of carriers, forwarders, agents and others to whom it may entrust the shipment.

CERTIFICATE OF ORIGIN—GENERIC

CERTIFICATE OF ORIGIN

© Copyright 1990 UNZ & CO.

The undersigned ___employee of owner_____
                                          (Owner or Agent, or Co.)

for _Universal Exports, 1700 West Washington Street, Phoenix, AZ 85007 U.S.A._____ declares
                          (Name and Address of Shipper)

that the following mentioned goods shipped on S/S _Sea-Land Explorer_____
                                                              (Name of Ship)

on the date of _December 12, 1995_____ consigned to __order of shipper_____

_____ are the product of the United States of America.

MARKS AND NUMBERS	NO. OF PKGS., BOXES OR CASES	WEIGHT IN KILOS		DESCRIPTION
		GROSS	NET	
As Addressed 1/10	10	455	435	1,000 textbooks as per Pro Forma Invoice dated September 1, 1995 VOID

Sworn to before me

this _17th_____ day of December_____ 19_95_____

_Pam Smith_____

My commission expires January 31, 1997

Dated at Phoenix_____ on the 17th____ day of Dec____ 19_95___

_____Joseph Reynolds_____
                (Signature of Owner or Agent)

The _Phoenix Area Chamber of Commerce_____, a recognized Chamber of Commerce under the laws of the State of

_AZ_____, has examined the manufacturer's invoice or shipper's affidavit concerning the origin of the merchandise and, according to the best of its knowledge and belief, finds that the products named originated in the United States of North America.

Secretary _John Black_____

CERTIFICATE OF ORIGIN—SPECIFIC FOR EXPORTS TO ISRAEL

© Copyright 1993 UNZ & CO.

U.S. CERTIFICATE OF ORIGIN
FOR EXPORTS TO ISRAEL

1. Goods consigned from exporter's business (name, address):	Reference No.
Universal Exports 1700 West Washington Street Phoenix, AZ 85007 U.S.A.	U.S.—ISRAEL FREE TRADE AREA CERTIFICATE OF ORIGIN (Combined declaration and certificate)

2. Goods consigned to (consignee's name, address)	
Israel Imports 1576 Haifa Street Tel Aviv, Israel	(See notes over leaf)

3. Means of transport and route (as far as known)	4. For official use
ocean Long Beach, CA, USA to Haifa	

5. Item number	6. Marks and numbers of packages	7. Number and kind of packages, description of goods	8. Origin criterion (see notes over leaf)	9. Gross Weight or other quantity	10. Number and date of invoices
1	As Addr. 1/10	10 cartons, textbooks	(a)	455 Kgs	9167 Jan 11,95

VOID

11. CERTIFICATION

The Phoenix Area Chamber of Commerce a recognized chamber of commerce, board of trade, or _____ under the laws of the State of AZ _____ has examined the manufacturer's invoice or shipper's affidavit concerning the origin of the merchandise and, according to the best of its knowledge and belief, finds that the products named originated in the United States of America.

John Black
Certifying Official

EXPORTER AS PRODUCER:

The undersigned hereby declares that he/she is the producer of the goods listed in this invoice and that they comply with the origin requirements specified for those goods in the U.S.—Israel Free Trade Area Agreement for goods exported to Israel.

Joseph Reynolds
Signature of Exporter

12. DECLARATION BY THE EXPORTER

The undersigned hereby declares that the above details and statements are correct; that all the goods were produced in the United States of America and that they comply with the origin requirements specified for those goods in the U.S.—Israel Free Trade Area Agreement for goods exported to Israel.

Joseph Reynolds
Signature of Exporter

Sworn to before me this 11th day of January 1995

Pam Smith
Signature of Notary Public

My commission expires Jan. 31, 1997

fully aware of it *before* the order gets to the letter of credit stage. If it is not mentioned to you, ask the importer if it is needed before you do the pro forma invoice. Legalization fees can range from a dollar or two from some consulates to as much as *3 percent of your total invoice* from Argentina's consulate. Your forwarder will advise you of fees. Depending on the time frames, you may need to use Federal Express or local messenger services.

EXPORT DOCUMENT CHECKLIST

Here is a rundown of the documents you'll need for exporting:

1. *Your commercial invoice*
2. *Your packing slip*
3. *Bill of lading: truck, ocean, air waybill*
4. *Shipper's export declaration*
   a) *If value is over USD 2,500 (except to Canada)*
   b) *If a validated license is required, regardless of value*
5. *Certificate of origin*
6. *Legalization, consularization or special documents*
7. *Postal:*
   a) *2966-A or 2966-B*
   b) *2976*

CANADA CUSTOMS INVOICE

On shipments valued at CD 1,200 or more (that's 1,200 *Canadian dollars*) the Canada Customs Invoice (see page 85) is required by your Canadian customer to present to Canadian customs. At today's rate of exchange, that is approximately USD 850.

Note that this form follows the same format as the shipper's export declaration. In fact, the supply houses have printed multicarbon forms so that with one typing you prepare both. These forms are now obsolete

unless you are shipping a licensed commodity, since the ex dec is generally not required for Canada, but my point is that since you know how to do an export declaration, you know how to do a Canada Customs Invoice. Here are the distinctions:

Field 5, Purchaser's Name and Address (if other than Consignee): Is the purchaser someone different from the consignee? If not, put in "N/A" or "same as consignee."

Field 6, Country of Transshipment: This usually doesn't apply because you will ship directly from the United States to Canada. But it is the same form for all Canadian imports and a Mexican firm selling to Canada normally transships through the United States.

Field 7, Country of Origin of Goods: This will probably be the United States. If you include some goods that were manufactured elsewhere, type in "see below" and put the name of the country of origin for each item down in column 12.

Field 8, Transportation: Mode (truck, air or ocean) and point of origination.

Field 9, Conditions of Sale and Terms of Payment: This covers the details of the sale. Is it FCA or CFR? Is it payment in advance or net thirty days?

Field 10, Currency of Settlement: Indicate whether you are being paid in U.S. dollars (USD) or Canadian dollars (CD).

The body of the Canada Customs Invoice is familiar to you, since it is the same as the export declaration except that net and gross weight are called for (in kilos). Gross weight is the total weight of the shipment. Net weight is the weight of the goods themselves, not counting the packing materials.

Field 19, Exporter's Name and Address (if other than Vendor): If you are the vendor, type in "same as vendor." If you are the vendor, but the goods are being shipped by

CANADA CUSTOMS INVOICE

Revenue Canada Customs and Excise	Revenu Canada Douanes et Accise	**CANADA CUSTOMS INVOICE** ***FACTURE DES DOUANES CANADIENNES***	Page 1 of 1 de

1. Vendor (Name and Address)/*Vendeur (Nom et adresse)*	2. Date of Direct Shipment to Canada/*Date d'expédition directe vers le Canada*

Universal Exports
1700 West Washington Street
Phoenix, AZ 85007 U.S.A.

January 5, 1996

3. Other References (Include Purchaser's Order No.)
Autres références (Inclure le n° de commande de l'acheteur)

Purchase Order 5678

4. Consignee (Name and Address)/*Destinataire (Nom et adresse)*	5. Purchaser's Name and Address (If other than Consignee) *Nom et adresse de l'acheteur (S'il diffère du destinataire)*

Canada Imports
1 Front Street West
Toronto, Ontario M5W 1A3
Canada

same as consignee

6. Country of Transhipment/*Pays de transbordement*

7. Country of Origin of Goods
Pays d'origine des marchandises
United States

IF SHIPMENT INCLUDES GOODS OF DIFFERENT ORIGINS ENTER ORIGINS AGAINST ITEMS IN 12
SI L'EXPEDITION COMPREND DES MARCHANDISES D'ORIGINES DIFFERENTES, PRÉCISER LEUR PROVENANCE EN 12

8. Transportation: Give Mode and Place of Direct Shipment to Canada
Transport: Préciser mode et point d'expédition directe vers le Canada

Truck ex Phoenix, AZ

9. Conditions of Sale and Terms of Payment
(i.e. Sale, Consignment Shipment, Leased Goods, etc.)
Conditions de vente et modalités de paiement
(p. ex. vente, expédition en consignation, location de marchandises, etc.)

F.O.B. Origin (Freight Collect)
Exporter's Invoice Paid in Advance

10. Currency of Settlement/*Devises du paiement*

USD

11. No. of Pkgs *N^{bre} de colis*	12. Specification of Commodities (Kind of Packages, Marks and Numbers, General Description and Characteristics, i.e. Grade, Quality) *Désignation des articles (Nature des colis, marques et numéros, description générale et caractéristiques, p. ex. classe, qualité)*	13. Quantity (State Unit) *Quantité* *(Préciser l'unité)*	14. Unit Price *Prix unitaire*	15. Total
10	cartons, as addressed, 1/10, 1,000 textbooks	X	10.00	10,000.00

VOID

18. If any of fields 1 to 17 are included on an attached commercial invoice, check this box *Si les renseignements des zones 1 à 17 figurent sur la facture commerciale, cocher cette boite* XX	16. Total Weight/*Poids Total*		17. Invoice Total *Total de la facture*
Commercial Invoice No./*N° de la facture commerciale* 1235	Net 435 Kg	Gross/*Brut* 455 Kg	10,000.00

19. Exporter's Name and Address (If other than Vendor) *Nom et adresse de l'exportateur (S'il diffère du vendeur)*	20. Originator (Name and Address)/*Expéditeur d'origine (Nom et adresse)*
same as vendor	Universal Exports 1700 West Washington Street Phoenix, AZ 85007 U.S.A.

21. Departmental Ruling (If applicable)/*Décision du Ministère (S'il y a lieu)* N/A	22. If fields 23 to 25 are not applicable, check this box *Si les zones 23 à 25 sont sans objet, cocher cette boite* ☐

23. If included in field 17 indicate amount: *Si compris dans le total à la zone 17, préciser:*	24. If not included in field 17 indicate amount: *Si non compris dans le total à la zone 17, préciser:*	25. Check (If applicable): *Cocher (S'il y a lieu):*
(i) Transportation charges, expenses and insurance from the place of direct shipment to Canada *Les frais de transport, dépenses et assurances à partir du point d'expédition directe vers le Canada* $ _____	(i) Transportation charges, expenses and insurance to the place of direct shipment to Canada *Les frais de transport, dépenses et assurances jusqu'au point d'expédition directe vers le Canada* $ collect	(i) Royalty payments or subsequent proceeds are paid or payable by the purchaser *Des redevances ou produits ont été ou seront versés par l'acheteur* ☐
(ii) Costs for construction, erection and assembly incurred after importation into Canada *Les coûts de construction, d'érection et d'assemblage après importation au Canada* $ _____	(ii) Amounts for commissions other than buying commissions *Les commissions autres que celles versées pour l'achat* $ not applicable	(ii) The purchaser has supplied goods or services for use in the production of these goods *L'acheteur a fourni des marchandises ou des services pour la production des marchandises* ☐
(iii) Export packing *Le coût de l'emballage d'exportation* $ 50.00	(iii) Export packing *Le coût de l'emballage d'exportation* $ _____	

DEPARTMENT OF NATIONAL REVENUE—CUSTOMS AND EXCISE   *MINISTÈRE DU REVENU NATIONAL—DOUANES ET ACCISE* someone else as exporter, that person's (or entity's) name and address go in this space.

Field 20, Originator: The originator might be you, or it could be someone else if you are, for example, acting as an export management company.

Fields 23 and 24: At the bottom, you must list specific dollar amounts for freight, insurance, packing, etc., and state whether they are included in the invoice total or will be charged extra. The reason is that if duty is payable (as there still is on many items of U.S. origin), your customer can deduct these charges from the total value on which he has to pay duty.

Field 25: If you are paying royalties back to Canada, or if the Canadian importer has supplied goods (materials) or services (blueprints, use of patents) for your use in manufacture, indicate this here.

Note again: Filling out this form is really not that difficult. If you run into problems, ask your Canadian importer, who can check with his Customs Broker, who deals with the form each day. Or call your freight forwarder. He will be glad to prepare it for you.

NAFTA CERTIFICATE OF ORIGIN

Under the North American Free Trade Agreement (NAFTA), a new Certificate of Origin (see page 87) is required for shipments entitled to special tariff treatment moving among Canada, Mexico and the United States.

"Special tariff treatment" means that the goods qualify for a lower or free duty rate. The situation you will probably run into most often is that of goods manufactured in one or more of the three countries, made from raw materials from one or more of the three countries. Examples are products made in the United States of U.S. and Mexican materials; products made in Mexico of U.S. and Canadian materials; and, of

course, goods made in one of the three countries, exclusively from that country's own raw materials, such as goods made in the United States of raw materials of U.S. origin.

The importer or his Customs Broker indicates the preferential treatment on the paperwork at the time of entry.

MORE ON NAFTA

A great deal of information is available on NAFTA and on trading with our NAFTA partners, Canada and Mexico. An excellent source, which includes dozens of reports on documentation and regulations as well as statistical data, is Flash Facts, from the U.S. Department of Commerce.

Call from any touch-tone telephone, and follow the instructions to input the numbers when requested. Input your fax number and the report you want is faxed directly to it, free of charge.

See the Resource List for phone numbers for Flash Facts (including a number for reports about trade with countries in the former Soviet Union).

The exporter is responsible for providing the importer with a completed and signed Certificate of Origin. Both exporter and importer are responsible for having a signed original certificate of origin on file for five years after the importation. The certificate is not given to the Customs Service at the time of shipment. It is kept on file by both the exporter and the importer and made available to the Customs Service on request.

Most of the form is very simple: names, addresses and Tax I.D. numbers. However, there are some distinctive characteristics about the certificate:

Field 2, Blanket Period: The certificate can be made out for one shipment at a time

NAFTA CERTIFICATE OF ORIGIN

DEPARTMENT OF THE TREASURY
UNITED STATES CUSTOMS SERVICE

Approved through 12/31/96
OMB No. 1515-0204

NORTH AMERICAN FREE TRADE AGREEMENT
CERTIFICATE OF ORIGIN

19 CFR 181.11, 181.22

1. Exporter Name and Address Universal Exports 1700 West Washington Street Phoenix, Arizona 85007 U.S.A. Tax I.D. Number 13-2345678	2. Blanket Period *(DD/MM/YY)* FROM 01/01/96 TO 31/12/96
3. Producer Name and Address SAME Tax I.D. Number	4. Importer Name and Address Ciudad de Libros SA de CV Av. Revolucion No. 1917 01040 Mexico DF Mexico Tax I.D. Number 12345

5. Description of Good(s)	6. HS Tariff Classification Number	7. Preference Criterion	8. Producer	9. Net Cost	10. Country of Origin
textbooks	4901.99	C	YES	NO	US

VOID

I Certify that:

- The information on this document is true and accurate and I assume the responsibility for proving such representations. I understand that I am liable for any false statements or material omissions made on or in connection with this document;

- I agree to maintain, and present upon request, documentation necessary to support this certificate, and to inform, in writing, all persons to whom the certificate was given of any changes that would affect the accuracy or validity of this certificate;

- The goods originated in the territory of one or more of the parties, and comply with the origin requirements specified for those goods in the North American Free Trade Agreement, and unless specifically exempted in Article 411 or Annex 401, there has been no further production or any other operation outside the territories of the Parties;

- This certificate consists of ___1___ pages, including all attachments.

11a. AUTHORIZED SIGNATURE *Joseph Reynolds*	11b. Company: Universal Exports
11c. NAME Joseph Reynolds	11d. Title: Export Manager
11e. DATE *(DD/MM/YY)* 01/01/96	11f. TELEPHONE NUMBER ▷ *(Voice)* (602) 555-2345 *(Facsimile)* (602) 555-5432

11.

or for a period of one year (a "blanket" certification). I recommend that you do blanket certifications (and if importing, request them), even if the shipment appears to be a one-time sale. If further shipments do materialize, your certificate is already done and on file.

For USD 1,000 or less, the exporter does not need a certificate of origin. The notation on the invoice will suffice.

Field 3, Producer's Name and Address and Tax I.D. Number: If you are the producer (same as exporter), indicate "same." If you are not the producer, indicate the appropriate information for the actual producer (or manufacturer). However, if you feel you need to keep this information confidential, you may write "available to Customs on request."

If you are not the producer of the goods, you must have information on file from the producer certifying the origin of the goods. This can be a NAFTA certificate of origin provided by your producer. The easy way, and just as acceptable is to get a letter on the producer's letterhead certifying the origin of the goods.

Field 6, HS Tariff Classification Number: This consists of the first six digits of the Harmonized Number (discussed under shipper's export declaration on page 78).

Field 7, Preference Criterion: NAFTA's five volumes contain pages of information about classification, favorable treatment and the paperwork involved.

The easiest products to classify turn out to be the same products you are most likely to buy and sell—products manufactured within Canada, Mexico and the United States, made of raw materials that originated in one or more of the three countries. Cut through all the fine print, and these products generally take the "C" preference criteria, as shown.

Agricultural goods are an exception, and there are other preference criteria for other situations. For example, goods assembled in one or more of the NAFTA countries from imported parts, such as parts from Japan assembled in Mexico into a completed product, are under different preference criteria. They stipulate that, for instance, 50 percent or more of the total net costs of the goods would have to be added for labor (or additional parts) provided within Canada, Mexico or the United States.

Field 8, Producer: Since Universal Exports is the producer of the books, fill in "Yes." Otherwise, it would be "No" (and the producer's information would be in field 3).

Field 9, Net Cost: This has to do with minimum requirements of Canada, Mexico or U.S. labor or parts on goods imported from elsewhere, as discussed above. In this case the product is made in the United States, so you say "No" to indicate that net cost doesn't apply.

Lengthy tomes are coming off the presses discussing the ins and outs of calculating some of these special preference criteria, including net cost, "transaction value" and other points. It is estimated that the various combinations and exceptions can yield more than one thousand possible rules of origin. The best recommendation I can give you is to see your freight forwarder if you export any product not 100 percent produced in NAFTA territory (Canada, Mexico and the United States) or if you have any questions.

Your freight forwarder will be glad to prepare a NAFTA certificate of origin, or any other documentation, at a nominal cost. (Freight forwarders are purchasing and studying the lengthy tomes.)

The form is being printed in English, Spanish and French versions. The information is the same in each field regardless of language, so a form in any language can be filed in any country.

HARBOR MAINTENANCE FEE

The harbor maintenance fee is your responsibility to file on export shipments. (On import, it is collected by U.S. Customs at the time of entry.)

Key points:

1. *It must be filed and paid each calendar quarter.*
2. *It must be received by U.S. Customs by the last day of the month following the close of the calendar quarter.*
3. *It does not apply to air, truck or rail shipments that do not use seaports.*
4. *You do not have to buy a particular form to file on, although several companies have forms available. You can file using your letterhead, or a plain piece of paper, using the format on page 90.*

EXPORT VESSEL MOVEMENT SUMMARY SHEET

If you are exporting by ocean, the Export Vessel Movement Summary Sheet is a form you must file with the U.S. Customs Service for each calendar quarter during the year. It is the basis for collecting a user's fee for using ports that are maintained by the U.S. government, based on ⅛ of 1 percent of the FAS value of your shipments (as shown on your shipper's export declarations).

The fee is due within the month following the close of the calendar quarter. So the form for the quarter October 1, 1995, through December 31, 1995, is due by January 31, 1996.

There is an official format for this summary sheet but no actual form for you to purchase. Following our sample, simply type the information on your letterhead.

Indicate your company's IRS number

(Employer Identification Number) or your Social Security number, and explain which it is.

Origin of Shipment is the seaport. If you are inland, indicate that, too, as Los Angeles via Phoenix.

Destination is the destination port, not necessarily the city to which your customer will eventually take the goods.

Commodity Code is your Schedule B number. If you have more than one on the export declaration, indicate the first one.

Value of Shipment, again, is FAS.

Total the shipment values for the quarter, multiply by 0.00125, sign and date, and send in the original with your check.

Note that you do not include shipments that left the United States by truck, railroad, air or postal service. The fee assessed here is for harbor maintenance, so only shipments using a harbor pay the fee.

Collection Class Code 502 is for export. Is the fee collected for import? Yes, but you do not file a quarterly report. The Customs Service collects the money at the time of importation along with any duties or other taxes payable. In fact, even if you take a cruise, you pay the user's fee in the price of your ticket for using the harbor on your way in and out.

POSTAL SERVICE FORMS

You will export by mail if you send samples or advertising material, perhaps in packages. (A prospective customer may ask for several sets of your catalog so she can send one to each of her sales representatives to get their reactions before ordering.)

For export shipments, there are two forms that look almost identical:

Form 2966-A (shown on page 91) has a peel-off back and adheres to the outside of the package.

Form 2966-B (shown on page 92 at top)

EXPORT VESSEL MOVEMENT SUMMARY SHEET FOR QUARTER

DATED FROM OCTOBER 1, 1995, TO DECEMBER 31, 1995

TO: U.S. Customs Service
        P.O. Box 70915
        Chicago, IL 60673-0915

FROM: Universal Exports   **Federal ID Number**
        1700 West Washington Street   55-1234567
        Phoenix, Arizona 85007

ORIGIN OF SHIPMENT	DESTINATION OF SHIPMENT	DATE OF ORIGIN	COMMODITY CODE	VALUE OF SHIPMENT
Long Beach via Phoenix	Yokohama	Dec 12 1995	4901.99.00102	$10,150.00

Total Value of Shipments for Quarter: $10,150.00

Collection Class Code 502

Total Fee Paid: ($10,150.00 × .00125) $12.69

CERTIFICATION

I hereby certify under penalties provided by law that the above information regarding cargo loaded for export subject to the harbor maintenance fee for the quarter ending December 31, 1995 is complete and accurate to the best of my knowledge.

Joseph Reynolds

January 31, 1996

---

is a form that makes an original and duplicate copy as you type it. Both the original and duplicate go into a plastic envelope (supplied free by the U.S. Postal Service), that has a peel-off back. Then the envelope is adhered to the outside of the package.

Which form do you use? It depends on the country and what the U.S. agreement is with that country. Next time you are at the post office, ask for some of each form and Publication 51, which lists every country in the world and tells you which form to use. It also lists the postage rates, weight limitations, etc.

While you are at the post office, ask for a sheet of 2976 labels (on page 92 at bottom). These gummed labels in sheet form are an abbreviated customs declaration, used for small, lightweight packages. There are also very low rates for small packages, both by air and by sea. Check Publication 51 for information on "Small Packets" before you mail a package overseas, and you will find yourself saving some money.

You can export via mail under a letter of credit. The letter of credit would call for a Certificate of Mailing stamped by the U.S. Postal Service as one of the required

U.S. POSTAL FORM #2966-A

United States Postal Service	No. 905413
From Expéditeur Universal Exports 1700 West Washington Street Phoenix, AZ 85007 U.S.A	**Sender's Instructions if parcel is undeliverable:** Dispositions de l'expéditeur En cas de non-livraison **[XX] Return to sender** Renvoyer à l'origine (NOTE: Parcel will be returned by surface and at sender's expense.) [ ] **Forward to:** Réexpédié à
TO Destinataire Japan Imports 147 Chuo-ku Yokohama, Japan	 [ ] **Abandon** Abandonné

QTY.	Itemized List of Contents Please Print	VALUE (US $)
5	catalogs	5.00

Signature of Sender *Joseph Reynolds*	Date Dec. 1, 1995

Insured No./Numéro d'assurance		Weight/Poids	
N/A		1 lbs.	6 ozs.

Insured Amount (US$)	Gold Francs	SDR/DTS	Postage
N/A	N/A	N/A	$18.75

PS Form 2966-A, June 1986   **Parcel Post Customs Declaration**
C2/CP3   **Colis de Poste Déclaration en Douane**

documents.

However, once you have mailed the package ... it's gone. You can't send a postal shipment "to order"; you can only address it to a specific consignee. So, if you do receive a letter of credit for a postal shipment, be very careful that there are no discrepancies anywhere.

Final notes on postal shipments: Remember that if your shipment has a value of $2,500 or over, or if it is a specifically licensable commodity (weapons, high-tech items, etc.), it requires a shipper's export declaration. If the commodity specifically requires a validated license, it requires a license for postal shipment just as it does for air, ocean or truck shipment.

I recommend that you include an invoice with each carton you ship. Put it in an envelope clearly marked "Invoice" and tape the envelope to the *outside* of the package. If you ship one order in more than one carton, tape an invoice on each carton because the cartons can easily get separated. Indicate "Carton 1 of 3 on order 4512," "Carton 2 of 3 on order 4512," etc.

U.S. POSTAL FORM #2966-B

DETACH STUB BEFORE MAILING

☆ U.S. GOVERNMENT PRINTING OFFICE: 1986 – 160-436

United States Postal Service	No. 434955

FROM Expéditeur

Universal Exports
1700 West Washington Street
Phoenix, AZ 85007 U.S.A.

Sender's Instructions
If parcel is undeliverable:

Dispositions de l'expéditeur
En cas de non-livraison

XX **Return to sender**
Renvoyer à l'origine
(NOTE: Parcel will be returned by surface and at sender's expense.)

☐ **Forward to:** Réexpédié à

TO Destinataire

Austria Imports
13 Hanovergasse
Wien, Austria

☐ **Abandon** Abandonné

QTY.	Itemized List of Contents Please Print	VALUE (US $)
5	catalogs	5.00

Signature of Sender *Joseph Reynolds*	Date Dec. 1, 1995

Insured No./Numéro d'assurance	Weight/Poids
N/A	1 lbs. 6 ozs.

Insured Amount (US$)	Gold Francs	SDR/DTS	Postage
N/A	N/A	N/A	$11.15

PS Form 2966-B, July 1986   **Parcel Post Customs Declaration**   Copy 1
C2/CP3   **Colis de Poste Déclaration en Douane**

FORM #2976 POSTAL LABEL

CUSTOMS—DOUANE C 1

May be Officially Opened
(Peut être ouvert d'office)

SEE INSTRUCTIONS ON BACK

Contents in detail:
Désignation détaillée
du contenu: _____

_____5 catalogs_____

_____

_____

_____

Mark X here if a gift . . . . ( )
Il s'agit d'un cadeau

or a sample of merchandise . . . . . ( )
d'un enchantillon de marchandises

Value: $5.00 Weight: 1# 6 oz
Valeur   Poids

PS Form 2976, Feb. 1989

BILL OF LADING CHARACTERISTICS

	CAN BE NEGOTIABLE	CAN BE ADDRESSED DIRECTLY
OCEAN	YES	YES
TRUCK	YES	YES
AIR	NO	YES
COURIER	NO	YES
POSTAL	NO	YES

INSURANCE POLICY

One final document involved is an insurance policy. This is prepared by the freight forwarder, who collects the premium and a service charge for preparing the policy. Study the example of an insurance policy on page 94; you will find it helpful to become familiar with the information required on such a policy.

INSURANCE

Generally, cargo insurance comes in three kinds:

All Risk: *This covers your cargo from door to door and covers partial as well as total loss or damage.*

With Average: *This covers your cargo for partial as well as total loss or damage on the main carrier only. For example, on a vessel shipment, it covers your cargo only from the time of loading onto the vessel to the time of unloading from the vessel. It does not include transportation to or from the piers or the time when the cargo is waiting on the pier.*

Free of Particular Average: *This covers your cargo only on the main carrier and covers only total loss or damage.*

Cost differences are not all that much; therefore, I recommend all risk coverage with this additional inexpensive coverage:

1. *War risk*
2. *S.R.C.C. (strikes, riots and civil commotions)*

Your freight forwarder can provide insurance coverage on a shipment-by-shipment basis, or you may choose to investigate obtaining a blanket policy on an annual basis. Your forwarder or business insurance carrier can furnish further information.

CERTIFICATE OF MARINE INSURANCE

$ __12,182.50__
(sum insured)

CERTIFICATE OF MARINE INSURANCE

No. 305735

WASHINGTON INTERNATIONAL INSURANCE COMPANY

1930 THOREAU DRIVE, SCHAUMBURG, IL. 60173
(708) 490-1850

This is to Certify, *That on the* 12th *day of* December   19 95 *, this Company*

insured under Policy No. M00001   *made for* Universal Exports

for the sum of Twelve Thousand One Hundred Eighty Two Dollars and 50/100 cents-- *Dollars,*

on Textbooks

Valued at sum insured. Shipped on board the *S/S or M/S* Sea-Land Explorer Voyage 12W   *and/or following steamer or steamers*

at and from Phoenix AZ   , *via* Long Beach CA
(Initial Point of Shipment)   (Port of Shipment)

to Yokohama, Japan   *and it is understood and agreed, that in case of loss, the same*
(Port or Place of Destination)

is payable to the order of Assured   *on surrender of this Certificate which conveys the right of collecting any such loss as fully as if the property were covered by a special policy direct to the holder hereof, and free from any liability for unpaid premiums. This certificate is subject to all the terms of the open policy, provided however, that the rights of a bona fide holder of this certificate for value shall not be prejudiced by any terms of the open policy which are in conflict with the terms of this certificate.*

SPECIAL CONDITIONS	MARKS & NUMBERS
NEW MERCHANDISE shipped subject to an UNDER DECK bill of lading insured– Against all risks of physical loss or damage from any external cause, irrespective of percentage, excepting those excluded by the F.C. & S. and S.R. & C.C. Warranties, arising during transportation between the points of shipment and of destination named herein. The above conditions apply only to New Approved Commodities, properly packed for export, as listed in the Master Policy to which this Certificate is made a part of. Commodities such as, but not limited to, Automobiles, Household Goods and Personal Effects, Wines, Liquors, Beer and Similar Spirits, are subject to further conditions and/or warranties of the policy. Non-approved commodities are subject to the F.P.A. conditions of the Master Policy unless broader conditions have been approved by these underwriters prior to attachment of risk and so endorsed hereon. All Risks, including S.R.C.C. and War Risks	As Addressed 1/10 Invoice 8124

USED MERCHANDISE AND/OR ON DECK SHIPMENTS (subject to an ON DECK bill of lading) insured– Warranted free of particular average unless caused by the vessel being stranded, sunk, burnt, on fire or in collision, but including risk of jettison and/or washing overboard, irrespective of percentage.	COMMODITY CODE Schedule B 4901.99.0010 2	COUNTRY CODE 588

TERMS AND CONDITIONS—SEE ALSO BACK HEREOF

WAREHOUSE TO WAREHOUSE: This insurance attaches from the time the goods leave the Warehouse and/or Store at the place named in the Policy for the commencement of the transit and continues during the ordinary course of transit, including customary transhipment if any, until the goods are discharged overside from the overseas vessel at the final port. Thereafter the insurance continues whilst the goods are in transit and/or awaiting transit until delivered to final warehouse at the destination named in the Policy or until the expiry of 15 days (or 30 days if the destination to which the goods are insured is outside the limits of the port) whichever shall first occur. The time limits referred to above to be reckoned from midnight of the day on which the discharge overside of the goods hereby insured from the overseas vessel is completed. Held covered at a premium to be arranged in the event of transhipment, if any, other than as above and/or in the event of delay in excess of the above time limits arising from circumstances beyond the control of the Assured.
NOTE–IT IS NECESSARY FOR THE ASSURED TO GIVE PROMPT NOTICE TO THESE ASSURERS WHEN THEY BECOME AWARE OF AN EVENT FOR WHICH THEY ARE "HELD COVERED" UNDER THIS POLICY AND THE RIGHT TO SUCH COVER IS DEPENDENT ON COMPLIANCE WITH THIS OBLIGATION.
PERILS CLAUSE: Touching the adventures and perils which this Company is contented to bear, and takes upon itself, they are of the seas, fires, assailing thieves, jettisons, barratry of the master and mariners, and all other like perils, losses and misfortunes (illicit or contraband trade excepted in all cases), that have or shall come to the hurt, detriment or damage of the said goods and merchandise, or any part thereof.
SHORE CLAUSE: Where this insurance by its terms covers while on docks, wharves or elsewhere on shore, and/or during land transportation, it shall include the risks of collision, derailment, overturning or other accident to the conveyance, fire, lightning, sprinkler leakage, cyclones, hurricanes, earthquakes, floods (meaning the rising of navigable waters), and/or collapse or subsidence of docks or wharves, even though the insurance be otherwise F.P.A.
BOTH TO BLAME CLAUSE: Where goods are shipped under a Bill of Lading containing the so-called "Both to Blame Collision" Clause, these Assurers agree as to all losses covered by this insurance, to indemnify the Assured for this Policy's proportion of any amount (not exceeding the amount insured) which the Assured may be legally bound to pay to the shipowners under such clause. In the event that such liability is asserted the Assured agrees to notify these Assurers who shall have the right at their own cost and expense to defend the Assured against such claim.
MACHINERY CLAUSE: When the property insured under this Policy includes a machine consisting when complete for sale or use of several parts, then in case of loss or damage covered by this insurance to any part of such machine, these Assurers shall be liable only for the proportion of the insured value of the part lost or damaged, or at the Assured's option, for the cost and expense, including labor and forwarding charges, of replacing or repairing the lost or damaged part; but in no event shall these Assurers be liable for more than the insured value of the complete machine.
LABELS CLAUSE: In case of damage affecting labels, capsules or wrappers, these Assurers, if liable therefor under the terms of this policy, shall not be liable for more than an amount sufficient to pay the cost of new labels, capsules or wrappers, and the cost of reconditioning the goods, but in no event shall these Assurers be liable for more than the insured value of the damaged merchandise.
DELAY CLAUSE: Warranted free of claim for loss of market or inherent vice or nature of the subject matter insured or for loss, damage or deterioration arising from delay, whether caused by a peril insured against or otherwise.
AMERICAN INSTITUTE CLAUSES: This insurance, in addition to the foregoing, is also subject to the following American Institute Cargo Clauses, current forms:

1. MARINE EXTENSION CLAUSES	4. CARRIER	7. INCHMAREE	10. SOUTH AMERICA 60 DAY CLAUSE
2. DEVIATION	5. BILL OF LADING, ETC.	8. CONSTRUCTIVE TOTAL LOSS	11. S.R. & C.C. ENDORSEMENT
3. CRAFT, ETC.	6. EXPLOSION	9. GENERAL AVERAGE	12. WAR RISK INSURANCE

PARAMOUNT WARRANTIES: THE FOLLOWING WARRANTIES SHALL BE PARAMOUNT AND SHALL NOT BE MODIFIED OR SUPERSEDED BY ANY OTHER PROVISION INCLUDED HEREIN OR STAMPED OR ENDORSED HEREON UNLESS SUCH OTHER PROVISION REFERS SPECIFICALLY TO THE RISKS EXCLUDED BY THESE WARRANTIES AND EXPRESSLY ASSUMES THE SAID RISKS:
F.C. & S.: Notwithstanding anything herein contained to the contrary, this insurance is warranted free from capture, seizure, arrest, restraint, detainment, confiscation, preemption, requisition or nationalization, and the consequences thereof or any attempt thereat, whether in time of peace or war and whether lawful or otherwise; also warranted free, whether in time of peace or war, from all loss, damage or expense caused by any weapon of war employing atomic or nuclear fission and/or fusion or other reaction or radioactive force or matter or by any mine or torpedo, also warranted free from all consequences of hostilities or warlike operations (whether there be a declaration of war or not), but this warranty shall not exclude collision or contact with aircraft, rockets or similar missiles or with any fixed or floating object (other than a mine or torpedo), stranding, heavy weather, fire or explosion unless caused directly (and independently of the nature of the voyage or service which the vessel concerned or, in the case of a collision, any other vessel involved therein, is performing) by a hostile act by or against a belligerent power; and for the purposes of this warranty 'power' includes any authority maintaining naval, military or air forces in association with a power.
Further warranted free from the consequences of civil war, revolution, rebellion, insurrection, or civil strife arising therefrom, or piracy.
NUCLEAR EXCLUSION: In the event that this Policy is extended to cover property prior to the attachment or subsequent to the expiration of the cover provided by the Marine Extension Clauses, such extension shall always be subject to the following exclusion unless specifically otherwise stated in writing by this company in the extension endorsement or otherwise.
This Company shall not be liable for any claim for loss, damage or expense arising directly or indirectly from any nuclear incident, reaction, radiation or any radioactive contamination, all whether controlled or uncontrolled, occurring while said property is within the United States, any territory of the United States, the Canal Zone or Puerto Rico, or arising from a source therein, and whether the loss, damage or expense be proximately or remotely caused thereby, or be in whole or in part caused by, contributed to, or aggravated by the peril(s) insured against in this Policy; however, subject to the foregoing and all provisions of this Policy, if this Policy insures against the peril of fire, then direct loss by fire resulting from nuclear incident, nuclear reaction, or radioactive contamination is insured against by this Policy.
S.R. & C.C.: Warranted free of loss or damage caused by or resulting from:
(a) strikes, lockouts, labor disturbances, riots, civil commotions, or the acts of any person or persons taking part in any such occurrences or disorders;
(b) vandalism, sabotage or malicious acts, which shall be deemed also to encompass the act or acts of one or more persons, whether or not agents of a sovereign power, carried out for political, terroristic or ideological purposes and whether any loss, damage or expense resulting therefrom is accidental or intentional.
TIME FOR SUIT: No suit or action against this Assurer for the recovery of any claim by virtue of this insurance shall be sustained in any Court of Law or Equity unless commenced within one (1) year from the time loss occurred or, if such limitation is not valid by the law of the place where the policy is issued, within the shortest contractual period of limitation permitted by such law.

This Certificate is issued in Original and Duplicate, one of which being accomplished the other to stand null and void.

To support a claim local Revenue Laws may require this certificate to be stamped.

Not transferable unless countersigned

Countersigned *Dan Richardson*   *Paul D. Amstutz*   *Lewis Walle*
                                        President   Secretary/Treasurer

ADDITIONAL CONDITIONS AND
INSTRUCTIONS TO CLAIMANTS ON REVERSE SIDE

ORIGINAL   W-13FF 11/93

CHAPTER NINE

Transportation Rates

- *Tariffs*

- *Containerization*

- *Truckload Shipment Rates*

- *Containerload Rates*

- *Air Shipment Rates*

- *Less-Than-Truckload Shipment Rates*

- *Beware Cargo NOS or NES*

To ship internationally, ocean, air, truck and rail are alternatives. Each means of transportation has its own rate structures, and each one has a series of books written about it. Here, I will cover some of the basic information about each type of freight rate.

I recommend that the first time you read through this chapter you concentrate on the basic themes; that is, the differences between the types of rating. I am not out to make a rate analyst of you. Later, when you are doing a pro forma invoice, or checking over a freight bill of your own, come back to this chapter and it will all make sense to you.

Your forwarder can do most of the rate work for you. But too many people in international trade do not understand the rates when they see them. Here is enough explanation to familiarize you with the rates you'll be working with.

A note about terminology: You'll notice that I use both the words *cargo* and *freight*. In general, *cargo* is the term used by maritime and sometimes by air freight people; *freight* is the term used by truckers and air freight people. Forwarders and brokers will call it whatever you call it.

TARIFFS

Truckers, steamship lines and airlines all publish rates in documents called *tariffs*, which may constitute a few pages or many volumes. They are generally available for perusal at a carrier's office, or you can pay to subscribe to them.

Rates can be obtained by calling the carrier direct or by contacting your freight forwarder. Most freight forwarders have a library of tariffs, these days often kept on computer disks or accessed by computer modem.

OBTAINING AN EXPORT RATE

Here is what you need to know to obtain an accurate export rate:

1. *What you are shipping.*
2. *Where it is going.*
3. *How much it weighs.*
4. *The dimensions.*
5. *The value.*
6. *The type of service (air, ocean, ground).*
7. *Any special requirements.*

CONTAINERIZATION

In modern-day shipping almost all air and ocean goods travel between destinations via containers. A container is a truck with a detachable chassis. Containerization has created a revolution in international shipping over the past generation, minimizing handling at port facilities.

Ocean Container

An ocean container is usually twenty feet or forty feet long and just under eight feet high and wide. (Your forwarder can give you exact dimensions for the steamship line you are using.)

If you load a full container shipment (see "Full Containerload Rates" on page 98), your forwarder will normally arrange for the container to be delivered to your premises, your "works," for loading. It will either be on its own chassis or on a flatbed truck and will have an identification number, usually four letters and seven numbers (ABCD 1234567).

After you have loaded the container, the trucker will move it either to the seaport or to a railroad "railhead" from which it will be shipped by rail to the seaport. At the seaport the container will be lifted by crane onto the vessel with other containers going to the same destination port. At the destination port, it will be lifted back onto a chas-

CONTAINER FLEET FOR SEA-LAND

This is the U.S. flag steamship line that in the 1960s was the innovator of ocean containers. Specifications for commonly used containers are below. Individual units may vary slightly, depending on manufacturer/purpose of the unit.

Dry Cargo 40-Foot

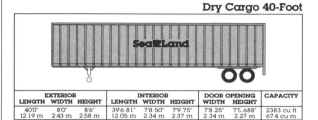

EXTERIOR			INTERIOR			DOOR OPENING		CAPACITY
LENGTH	WIDTH	HEIGHT	LENGTH	WIDTH	HEIGHT	WIDTH	HEIGHT	
40'0"	8'0"	8'6"	39'6.81"	7'8.50"	7'9.75"	7'8.25"	7'5.688"	2383 cu ft
12.19 m	2.43 m	2.58 m	12.05 m	2.34 m	2.37 m	2.34 m	2.27 m	67.4 cu m

Dry Cargo 20-Foot

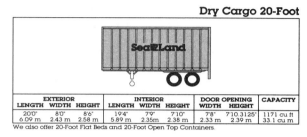

EXTERIOR			INTERIOR			DOOR OPENING		CAPACITY
LENGTH	WIDTH	HEIGHT	LENGTH	WIDTH	HEIGHT	WIDTH	HEIGHT	
20'0"	8'0"	8'6"	19'4"	7'9"	7'10"	7'8"	7'10.3125"	1171 cu ft
6.09 m	2.43 m	2.58 m	5.89 m	2.35m	2.38 m	2.33 m	2.39 m	33.1 cu m

We also offer 20-Foot Flat Beds and 20-Foot Open Top Containers.

Dry Cargo High Cube 40-Foot

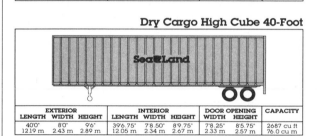

EXTERIOR			INTERIOR			DOOR OPENING		CAPACITY
LENGTH	WIDTH	HEIGHT	LENGTH	WIDTH	HEIGHT	WIDTH	HEIGHT	
40'0"	8'0"	9'6"	39'6.75"	7'8.50"	8'9.75"	7'8.25"	8'5.75"	2687 cu ft
12.19 m	2.43 m	2.89 m	12.05 m	2.34 m	2.67 m	2.33 m	2.57 m	76.0 cu m

Dry-Cargo High-Cube 45-Foot

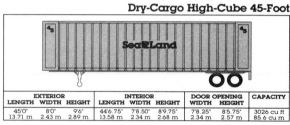

EXTERIOR			INTERIOR			DOOR OPENING		CAPACITY
LENGTH	WIDTH	HEIGHT	LENGTH	WIDTH	HEIGHT	WIDTH	HEIGHT	
45'0"	8'0"	9'6"	44'6.75"	7'8.50"	8'9.75"	7'8.25"	8'5.75"	3026 cu ft
13.71 m	2.43 m	2.89 m	13.58 m	2.34 m	2.68 m	2.34 m	2.57 m	85.6 cu m

Reefer Cargo 40-Foot

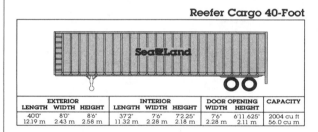

EXTERIOR			INTERIOR			DOOR OPENING		CAPACITY
LENGTH	WIDTH	HEIGHT	LENGTH	WIDTH	HEIGHT	WIDTH	HEIGHT	
40'0"	8'0"	8'6"	37'2"	7'6"	7'2.25"	7'6"	6'11.625"	2004 cu ft
12.19 m	2.43 m	2.58 m	11.32 m	2.28 m	2.18 m	2.28 m	2.11 m	56.0 cu m

Reefer Cargo High Cube 40-Foot

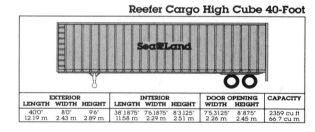

EXTERIOR			INTERIOR			DOOR OPENING		CAPACITY
LENGTH	WIDTH	HEIGHT	LENGTH	WIDTH	HEIGHT	WIDTH	HEIGHT	
40'0"	8'0"	9'6"	38'1.875"	7'6.1875"	8'3.125"	7'5.3125"	8'.875"	2359 cu ft
12.19 m	2.43 m	2.89 m	11.58 m	2.29 m	2.51 m	2.26 m	2.45 m	66.7 cu m

Open Top 40-Foot

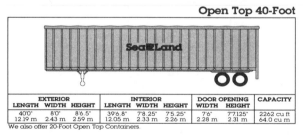

EXTERIOR			INTERIOR			DOOR OPENING		CAPACITY
LENGTH	WIDTH	HEIGHT	LENGTH	WIDTH	HEIGHT	WIDTH	HEIGHT	
40'0"	8'0"	8'6.5"	39'6.8"	7'8.25"	7'5.25"	7'6"	7'7.125"	2262 cu ft
12.19 m	2.43 m	2.59 m	12.05 m	2.33 m	2.26 m	2.28 m	2.31 m	64.0 cu m

We also offer 20-Foot Open Top Containers.

Flat Bed 40-Foot

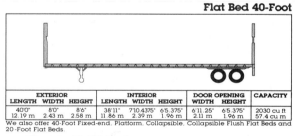

EXTERIOR			INTERIOR			DOOR OPENING		CAPACITY
LENGTH	WIDTH	HEIGHT	LENGTH	WIDTH	HEIGHT	WIDTH	HEIGHT	
40'0"	8'0"	8'6"	38'11"	7'10.4375"	6'5.375"	6'11.25"	6'5.375"	2030 cu ft
12.19 m	2.43 m	2.58 m	11.86 m	2.39 m	1.96 m	2.11 m	1.96 m	57.4 cu m

We also offer 40-Foot Fixed-end, Platform, Collapsible, Collapsible Flush Flat Beds and 20-Foot Flat Beds.

Chassis 40/45-Foot

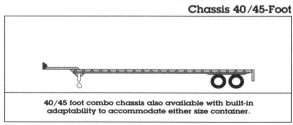

40/45 foot combo chassis also available with built-in adaptability to accommodate either size container.

sis, a flatbed truck, or a flatbed rail car; clear customs; and move on to its final destination. The empty container is picked up and returned to a Container Yard, sometimes called a CY.

If you have a shipment that is less than a containerload (see "Less-Than-Container-load Rates," page 101), your forwarder will ask you to deliver your shipment to a container freight station (CFS), usually in the port city, where it will be loaded with other shipments into a container for shipping on to its destination.

Air Container

Air shipments can move by container, too, although the container sizes are smaller than those for ocean shipments. Some of even the largest capacity air cargo containers can be released to your premises for loading and, after shipment, to the consignee's premises for unloading. The containers are designed to fit the interior configuration of cargo jets or the cargo bellies of passenger jets.

Normally, you won't directly load a container, but your shipment will be consolidated at the airline's terminal with other shipments to make up a containerload shipment.

Ocean containers are truckload shipments, so let's summarize how truckload shipments work.

TRUCKLOAD SHIPMENT RATES

Most truckload shipments that move interstate, as well as most that move within a state (intrastate), are figured in cents per mile with a maximum allowable weight, such as "400 miles at 162 cents per mile, $648.00 total with a maximum allowable weight of 40,000 pounds."

Sometimes you may ship to the port via truckload, and the goods will be transferred there into a container, although this in-

volves extra handling. A normal domestic truck semitrailer is approximately 7½ feet by 7½ feet by 40, 42 or 48 feet long. Sometimes "pups," which are 27½ feet long, are used; the rate for these is usually less than for a full truckload.

The rate quoted may be for "general commodities," meaning pretty much anything that is not hazardous or perishable and hence does not require special handling, or it may be a particular rate for a particular commodity.

REDUCING SHIPPING COSTS

Probably the single most important thing to remember about shipping is that it costs money to ship air—the more you can condense your packing, the more you can save on freight charges.

CONTAINERLOAD RATES

Ocean shipping rates are generally figured in terms of full containerload or less-than-containerload. The sample on page 99 gives steamship tariff rates for both.

Full Containerload Rates

Rates for full containerload (FCL) can be expressed as:

From California, U.S.A., Ports to Ports of Japan
Textbooks, in cartons
20-foot container   USD 1,416.00
40-foot container   USD 1,900.00

Generally, a 40-foot container can be moved much more inexpensively than two 20-foot containers. It is the same amount of freight but much less handling because there is only one real shipment, one set of documents, etc.

Highway and steamship safety regulations usually impose a maximum weight that you are permitted to load on board a

SAMPLE STEAMSHIP TARIFF

U.S. outbound rates from the Pacific coast ports of the United States on the one hand, to the ports of Japan and South Korea on the other hand, in U.S. dollars, per 1,000 kg or 1 cubic meter, whichever results in the greater revenue.

	20-FOOT CONTAINER	40-FOOT CONTAINER	LCL
Books, Textbooks, and Others, Hard or Softbound, in Cartons	1416	1900	261 W/M
Calendars	1416	1900	220 W/M
Cardboard for Artist's Use, Colored or Noncolored	1375	1775	199 W/M
Cardboard for Industrial Use	1300	1675	189 W/M
Cargo, NOS	1875	2247	310 W/M
Currency Adjustment Factor	300	400	39%
Fuel Adjustment Factor	48	60	3 W/M
Origin Receiving Charge	341	380	29 W/M

Effective August 1, 1995

container. But other than that, the container is yours and you can load it as you please. As a trucker would say, "Nose to tail, side to side, floor to ceiling."

The approximate interior dimensions of ocean containers are shown on the chart on page 97. They vary slightly from manufacturer to manufacturer.

If you plan to do ocean shipping by container, you should be familiar with the shipping cartons you will be using. You should also be able to calculate how many cartons will fit on board a container. Many of your consignees will ask you for a pro forma invoice based on a "20-foot containerload," expecting that you will be able to determine better than they how much product will fit on board.

Sometimes there is extra space. If your cartons are 16″×16″×16″, they will only stack five high, leaving just short of a foot of unusable space. New cartons may be a possibility. Or perhaps you have an additional product in smaller cartons that you can encourage containerload purchasers to buy to "ship free." That is, once you have

paid the freight for the principal product, there are no additional freight charges for the "ship free" merchandise.

Terminal Receiving Charges

In addition to ocean freight, there may be terminal receiving charges (TRCs) or origin receiving charges. These charges for loading the container on the vessel were covered in chapter five, since they are charges that the exporter becomes responsible for on shipments beyond FAS, FOB, CFR, CIF, etc.

For full containerload shipments, TRCs are usually expressed as either:

- Flat, as "$341.00 per 20-foot container, $380.00 per 40-foot container"; or
- Rated, as "$17.25 per 1,000 kilos" or "$29.00 per cubic meter."

So you may need to deal with metric measurements to calculate ocean freight rates.

Calculating the Rate

The 1,000 kilos is easy. It is sometimes called a kiloton because it is the metric version of our ton. A kilo is 2.24 pounds, so a kiloton of 1,000 kilos is 2,240 pounds. If you have 22,400 pounds of goods on board a container, you have 10 kilotons of goods. If you pay $17.25 per 1,000 kilos for TRCs, this comes to $172.50 ($17.25 × 10). For 455 kilos, this is $7.85 ($17.25 × 0.455).

A cubic meter is 35.32 cubic feet, but here is the easy way to figure cubic meters. Since you are used to measuring in inches and feet, tally up the total cubic feet in the container. Let's say this comes to 950 cubic feet, allowing that you did not load every single cubic inch of the container solid with cargo. (Truckers refer to the air as shipping "sailboat fuel.")

Multiply the 950 cubic feet by 0.029 to get cubic meters. In this case, that is 27.55 cubic meters, which you can abbreviate as 27.55M3 (Don't use CM, since that means centimeters.)

So if you have 1.09 M3 of cargo on board, and you are charged $29.00 per cubic meter, the TRC comes to $31.61 (1.09 × $29.00).

In these examples the TRCs are $7.85 based on a tariff that tells us to figure the TRCs based on weight and $31.61 based on capacity used. In some steamship tariffs, you must figure both possibilities for a given shipment because the tariff will read, "$17.25 per 1,000 kilos or $29.00 per cubic meter, whichever results in the greater revenue to the carrier." Almost all commodities rate at a higher revenue based on capacity (cubic meters) than by weight. Unless you are shipping some extremely dense products (barbells, anvils, steel bars, some chemicals), you are going to find yourself paying based on the cubic capacity or "cube."

Importers pay an unloading charge at destination, usually called DDC for destination delivery charge.

Fuel Prices

Some additional charges may apply to your containerload shipment, one of which relates to the price of fuel. Fuel surcharges come and go, depending on the supply of and demand for oil, which fluctuate with world conditions. When Iraq invaded Kuwait in 1992, fuel prices went up. Rather than revise and republish every tariff, the steamship lines published an additional page, which said something like "Fuel Adjustment Factor of 5% in effect for 30 days" or "Fuel Adjustment Factor of $48.00 per 20-foot container and $60.00 per 40-foot container in effect for 30 days." At the end of that time, the fee was revised upward or downward, continued or discontinued, enabling the rates to float up and down as the price of fuel fluctuated. Most, if not all, truckers also instituted temporary fuel surcharges during the Persian Gulf War.

Sometimes you will see the fuel fee abbreviated FSC for *fuel surcharge*, and sometimes you will see it abbreviated BSC for *bunker surcharge*. That goes back to the days when bunkers of coal were loaded on board a vessel for fuel.

FSC charges may be stated as flat per container, as percentages, or in terms of weight or measure or both ("Fuel Surcharge of $3.00 per Cubic Meter or $5.65 per kiloton").

Exchange Rates of the U.S. Dollar

As the U.S. dollar fluctuates in relation to other currencies, a steamship line's revenue can vary depending on what currency it is being paid with. If the dollar fluctuates downward, a steamship line files a tariff page with a surcharge for people paying in U.S. dollars on both export and import shipments. Such a currency adjustment factor (CAF) might be filed as:

"Currency Adjustment Factor of 39% in

effect for 30 days for payment in U.S. dollars."

CAF charges, like fuel surcharges, may be per container, by percentage, or by weight or measure or both.

Less-Than-Containerload Rates

If you ship via ocean and don't have a full containerload (known as LCL, or less-than-containerload), you would ship to the container freight station (CFS) maintained by the steamship line in the port city. There your shipment would be accepted and combined with other outbound shipments in an ocean container to the same port for ease of handling and safety of the goods.

For LCL shipments almost all rates are expressed in terms of both weight and measure and by type of commodity. You might find a rate from Los Angeles to Yokohama reading:

"$261.00 per cubic meter or metric ton, whichever results in the greater revenue."

Here, the rate factor is the same either way; it is a question of whether to base it on cube or weight. Sometimes you may find it expressed as two different rate factors:

"$261.00 per Cubic Meter or $225.00 per Metric Ton, whichever results in the greater revenue."

As discussed above, most products are rated according to the cube, rather than according to the weight. On LCL especially, you may occasionally run into a carrier who quotes rates as: "$261.00 per 2240 or 40, whichever results in the greater revenue." This is a way of quoting rates in the U.S. system, while keeping close to the metric sizes: "2240" means 2,240 pounds, or a metric ton expressed in pounds; "40" means forty cubic feet, a rounded-off cubic-foot version of the cubic meter.

You may find fuel surcharges or currency adjustment factors at given times.

Also, a particular port or steamship line may have additional charges. A steamship line always charges a minimum, usually $75 to $150 per shipment or "per bill of lading." The reason, of course, is that if you shipped an extremely small amount of cargo, say one cubic foot weighing 25 pounds, the carrier couldn't begin to recover the cost of handling the shipment.

That summarizes ocean rating. Your forwarder will be glad to find rates for you as well as do the math if you supply cubes and weights. Cubic feet and pounds are OK also; the forwarder will do the conversion.

After you have done a few pro forma invoices and a few shipments and have seen some ocean bills of lading rated with your product on board, you will find it very easy to understand all the ocean rates you see.

TRANSSHIPMENT

Transshipment can mean more than one thing.

One meaning is for the shipment to leave one country and cross a second en route to a third. For example, trucks from Canada bound for Mexico cross the United States all the time.

A second meaning is for a shipment to change vessels at an intermediate port en route to its final destination, but under one bill of lading. For example, ABC steamship line issues a bill of lading from Los Angeles to Keelung, Taiwan, but the ship only goes back and forth between Los Angeles and Singapore. At Singapore the shipment is unloaded and put on another vessel that sails between Singapore and Keelung. At Keelung the shipment is unloaded and available for the importer to claim under the original ABC bill of lading.

This is a routine matter. Sometimes the second vessel belongs to the same steamship line and sometimes it belongs to another steamship line that runs just the second leg of the trip. The key is that the originating steamship line's

---

INTERNATIONAL AIRLINE CARGO TARIFF GENERAL COMMODITIES

Item 213A

U.S. outbound rates from Phoenix, Arizona
Currency: U.S. Dollars
Rate per Kilogram

TO:	MINIMUM	TO: 49 Kgs	50-99	100-299	300-499	500+
Hong Kong	75.00	4.65	3.98	3.87	3.82	3.76
Seoul	75.00	4.52	3.83	3.68	3.60	3.45
Tokyo	75.00	4.43	3.83	3.65	3.50	3.43

Rates are air freight airport-to-airport, not including pickup, delivery, forwarding fees or Customs clearance.

Effective: June 1, 1995

---

original bill of lading is used to claim the shipment at destination.

Letters of credit routinely prohibit transshipments in cases where a second bill of lading is issued for a second steamship line (the third meaning). But it is still up to the buyer (importer) whether to permit it or not.

AIR SHIPMENT RATES

Air shipments are much easier than ocean shipments because they are consistently rated in kilos. The chart above shows tariff rates for air shipments.

Divide your shipment's weight in pounds by 2.24, and you have kilos. Multiply it by the rate given in the tariff.

An air shipment of 224 pounds is 100 kilos. With a rate of $7.65 per kilo from Phoenix to Tokyo, that comes to $765 for textbooks. Easy enough! Air rates usually apply to a specific commodity.

Sometimes you will see fuel and currency adjustments in air freight, but an air carrier's tariffs are much smaller and less complicated than a steamship line's tariffs. So they are more inclined to publish a new tariff with the change included.

Airlines also have COD service, although it is limited when it comes to international shipments. It is generally available to Canada and sometimes to other countries.

Dimensional Weight

One important thing to watch out for on air freight is *dimensional weight*, which applies if you ship cargo that is not very dense. Suppose instead of a shipment of textbooks, you are shipping a crate of loose feathers for making pillows. The crate is 60″×60″×60″, so it is a fairly large crate. But because it contains loose feathers, it only weighs 200 pounds. While air freight rates are not, strictly speaking, set up on a weight and measure basis, the air carrier will not let you ship a crate that size and pay for only 200 pounds. You must pay for a minimum number of pounds based on the cubic inches. Typically, this is a minimum of one pound for every 166 cubic inches of cargo.

Not hard to figure—take the dimensions of the crate in inches and multiply: 60″×60″×60″=216,000 cubic inches. Divide 216,000 cubic inches by the factor of 166 to get the minimum number of pounds for which you will be charged: 1,301.2 pounds. The carrier usually rounds it up, to 1,302 pounds. If the rate is $6.50 per kilo, divide 1,302 pounds by 2.24 to get 581.25. Round up to 582 kilos and multiply by $6.50 to get $3,783.00. That is the charge.

Note that this is the *minimum* charge. If the crate weighed more, say 1,250 kilograms, then you would be charged for that. Here, you would have $6.50 per kilo times 1,250 kilograms, or $8,125.

Air freight rates drop per kilo as the size of the shipment goes up. So a shipment of 49 kilos and under is rated as $8.75 per kilo with a minimum charge of $75. From 50 kilos to 99 kilos, the charge is $8.10 per kilo and so on.

LESS-THAN-TRUCKLOAD SHIPMENT RATES

As "LCL" means less-than-containerload for an ocean shipment, "LTL" means less-than-truckload for a truck shipment. If you ship to Canada or Mexico via truckload you will usually be quoted a flat rate for origin to destination for the entire truckload. But sending less-than-truckload shipments to a port city is a completely different matter. LTL rates are quoted "per cwt.", meaning "per hundredweight" or "per hundred pounds." As the trucking industry has grown, a rating system has been established based on a book called the *National Motor Freight Classification*.

You do not need to buy this book, and most libraries do not have it, but you should know about it. Probably only a couple of pages will apply to you, and your trucking company can give you copies of these pages, as well as the tariff pages that apply to your shipment, whether it is the domestic part of an international shipment or a domestic shipment by itself. (Many of the larger companies can provide you with a complete national tariff covering all classes from all points to all points on two computer disks, at no charge.)

All LTL truckers work according to this book. It lists a classification number and a "class" for everything under the sun. From the class, you determine a rate from point A to point B for the commodity.

The textbooks in the example weigh 1,000 pounds and are class 65. Check the tariff page for Phoenix to Long Beach, the port to which you must deliver, and find the rate for class 65 for a 1,000 pound shipment: $16.17 per 100 pounds. Multiply by ten (1,000 pounds = ten hundredweights). Note that there is a minimum charge. So the 1,000-pound shipment comes to $161.17 without any discounts (see sidebar).

Truckers sometimes charge extra for a pier delivery, but the LTL shipment may not be going to a pier. The CFS may be a warehouse downtown. Truckers also charge additional for special services, such as delivery by appointment, special equipment needed, or COD service.

A tariff, or rate chart, from a trucking company to show how rates are calculated for LTL is shown on page 104.

DISCOUNTS

Since truck deregulation, all LTL truckers have initiated discount programs. The tariff rate applies to everyone, but the better the customer (inbound or outbound), the higher the discount the company will put in for you.

In reality, I have never known anyone not to get at least a 15 percent to 20 percent discount, even as a brand new customer, just by asking for it. So if you are not getting an LTL discount, see your trucking company's representative. If you still don't get one, see another trucking company's representative.

TRUCKING COMPANY'S RATES FOR CALCULATING LTL SHIPMENTS

TRANS-PORT EXPRESS TARIFF
Effective January 1, 1995 from points in Phoenix, Arizona, to:

ZIP	CLASS	MINIMUM CHARGE	LESS THAN 500 LBS.	500 LBS. +	1,000 LBS. +	5,000 LBS. +
90801	55	79.11	19.79	17.02	15.04	9.50
	65	79.11	21.27	18.29	16.17	10.21
	70	79.11	22.21	19.10	16.89	10.66
	85	79.11	25.59	22.01	19.45	12.29
	100	79.11	29.76	25.59	22.62	14.29
	125	79.11	37.42	32.18	28.45	17.97
	150	79.11	45.01	38.71	34.22	21.61

All charges in dollars and cents per hundred lbs. (cwt.) except for minimum charge, which is per shipment.

Truck Shipments to Canada

I mentioned COD service, which means the trucker is responsible for collecting your invoice upon delivery. This doesn't apply if you ship to a steamship line, of course, but it can apply if you ship direct to your Canadian customer.

Many of the larger U.S. companies operate daily service into Canada, either through a subsidiary company or through an "interline" company with whom they have working agreements to handle the freight and split the profits.

Most of them do provide COD service to Canada, which can require that the customer pay, as you direct, either by: (1) his own (company) check, or (2) cash or certified check, before his shipment is released to him. Be sure you indicate United States dollars or Canadian dollars on your invoice as well as on the trucker's paperwork. I recommend that it be spelled out and not abbreviated in this case, so there are no mistakes at the time of delivery.

Of course, on a COD shipment, if you are going to require cash or certified check, be sure your customer knows in advance. In addition to COD service, most of the larger U.S. truckers provide both prepaid (you pay the freight) and collect (they pay the freight) service, without collecting your invoice. Rating is either truckload or LTL as described above.

Truck Shipments to Mexico

Mexico is a different story. For various reasons, U.S. truckers do not run into Mexico. However, the major truckers and many regional firms run to gateways at the border: Tijuana, California; Nogales, Arizona; El Paso, Laredo and Brownsville, Texas.

The easiest way to ship to a Mexican point is to quote your customer DAF (delivered at frontier) the border crossing city of his choice, and let his Customs Broker at the border make arrangements for moving the freight across the border, clearing customs, and forwarding the goods on to destination.

DAF is the same as CFR except that instead of shipping the goods to the destination city (CFR Mexico City), you ship the goods to the buyer's agent (Customs Broker) at the frontier—or border—city of his choice (DAF Nogales, Arizona, U.S.A.)

Generally, a cargo insurance policy is not purchased for DAF shipments. As far as the exporter is concerned, these are domestic shipments until delivered. So you have a right to file your claim against the trucker for your full cost of the goods in the event of loss or damage.

On the Mexican side, it is again a domestic shipment. Most Mexican firms are used to such arrangements. The United States is Mexico's largest supplier as well as its best customer, and Mexican firms are aware of the arrangements that need to be made at the border. Firms that import regularly generally have a Customs Broker permanently retained at their most convenient border crossing.

BEWARE CARGO NOS OR NES

Cargo NOS means *Cargo Not Otherwise Specified*. Sometimes you will find *Cargo NES* meaning *Cargo Not Elsewhere Specified*, usually in steamship tariffs. These terms are used if no one has shipped your commodity before, or not enough of it, or not with this steamship line, so no rate has been established for the particular commodity. The NOS and NES rates are very, very high catchall rates.

If a rate is quoted to you as NOS or NES, you should immediately get together with your forwarder and/or a representative of the steamship line to establish an appropriate rate for the commodity.

CHAPTER TEN

Alternative Concepts for Exporting or Importing

- *Intermodal Service*

- *Air Freight and Consolidations*

- *Foreign Sales Corporations*

- *Countertrade*

- *Protections and Guarantees*

So far, everything has been straightforward. Apples are red and oranges are orange. Now, we'll look at some hybrids to come up with some valuable answers to important questions:

- Can I ship FCA from an inland U.S. city? (Yes.)
- How do I import goods CIP an inland U.S. city? (Easy.)
- Are there special tax advantages to exporting? (Yes, indeed.)

These are valuable points many books on international trade do not cover. My objective here is to make this one chapter worth the price of the whole book to you.

INTERMODAL SERVICE

Intermodal service uses more than one means of transportation—generally rail-and-ocean or truck-and-ocean—under one bill of lading. Most shipments do move by more than one means of transportation, but here I'm referring to two specific types of service: the landbridge and the Non-Vessel Operating Common Carrier, or NVOCC.

Shipping Via Landbridges

Landbridges are two types of shipments— the microbridge and the minibridge—that can offer economical solutions to specific transportation situations.

Microbridges

When we discussed terms of sale and the pro forma invoice in earlier chapters, I mentioned that you can ship FCA even from an inland city. This is done through a *microbridge*.

Steamship rates have historically been quoted from a seaport to a seaport. In recent years, an invention called the microbridge has come about. Microbridge rates cover shipping from a city that is not a sea-

port via a city that is a seaport to a foreign city, such as Phoenix to Tokyo via Los Angeles. The shipment originates in Phoenix, which is not a seaport, via Los Angeles, which is, to Tokyo, which is. Some other examples: Salt Lake City to Tokyo via Los Angeles; Salt Lake City to Le Havre via New York City; Phoenix to Rotterdam via Galveston.

In these instances, the steamship line quotes a rate for shipments originating in the inland city, being shipped by truck or train to the U.S. seaport, and then by ship to the foreign city. They take the shipment "in charge" in your city, so you receive a rate of *X* dollars to cover your shipment from Phoenix to Tokyo, or from Salt Lake City to Le Havre.

You deliver your shipment to the local CFS or pull an empty container from the local CY and return it there loaded. Or the steamship line will include the local cartage in its rate.

Notice that this lets you ship FOB your city just as if it were an ocean seaport: You pay for the forwarding and the local cartage only. Or, if you are some distance from the nearest microbridge city, you pay the trucking to that city.

For importers this can operate in reverse: Goods are shipped from Le Havre into Salt Lake City, where the importer can claim the goods and arrange customs clearance. This is a purchase made by the Utah importer, CIP Salt Lake City.

WHAT IS INTERMODAL SHIPPING?

Intermodal *shipping simply means that more than one mode is used in transport: container shipments that move truck-rail-ocean, for example.*

Many nationwide trucking companies have entered into the less-than-containerload ocean shipping business. They arrange for their truck to make the pickup at your door and move the shipment via their own NVOCC. They can offer a through-rate to the final port, and, in some cases, can offer your customer customs clearance and delivery service. You still choose your own forwarder to arrange documentation, insurance, etc.

Minibridges

Minibridges are tariffs from a city that is a port to a city that is a port via a city that is a port.

For example: You are in Los Angeles and have a shipment to Le Havre, France. Both cities are ports. The steamship line you use may sail to France only out of Gulf and Atlantic ports but be all set up to take the goods in charge in Los Angeles, move them by rail to Galveston, and then load them on the steamship to Le Havre.

In this instance, you save the time of going through the Panama Canal, and the rate from Los Angeles may be very attractive, since the steamship line providing this service competes with other lines sailing from the West Coast.

INTERMODAL SERVICE TO CANADA AND MEXICO

Shipping to and receiving from Canada by truck has been easy for years with most of the larger trucking companies. Your local trucking company representative can give you full information. Some U.S. trucking companies operate Canadian subsidiaries, others have working partnerships with Canadian companies.

With the implementation of NAFTA, many companies are jumping on the intermodal bandwagon. You can now ship from U.S. cities to Mexican cities with one-company responsibility and one confirmed rate quotation for full truckload and less-than-truckload shipments.

You can also bring shipments in by truck

from Mexican points, handling the routing from the U.S. end.

These networks usually work via U.S. trucking companies in a partnership arrangement with Mexican trucking companies.

Steamship Lines Without Steamships: The NVOCC

The NVOCC (Non-Vessel Operating Common Carrier) can take landbridges one step further. These are literally international ocean carriers that do not operate their own vessels.

How does this work? Let's say you and I are preparing to start an NVOCC. We will provide service from Los Angeles to and from Tokyo because we have a working relationship with a company that will act as our agent there.

We make an agreement with a steamship line, or lines, that we will guarantee a certain amount of freight per week, perhaps ten containers in each direction each week. We will pay for these containers whether we use them or not, and sign a contract for a year. Naturally, since we are instantly very good customers of the steamship line, they will, upon request, give us extremely competitive rates for what we will list as FAK (freight, all kinds).

After satisfying the Federal Maritime Commission's requirements, we now publish our own tariff and hold ourselves open to the public for shipments to and from Tokyo. We are, in essence, buying space wholesale and selling it retail. We will operate our own CFS in Los Angeles and bring empty containers from the steamship line to be loaded, fill them, and send them to our agent in Tokyo. The Tokyo agent will separate the contents into individual shipments again and make them available for customers to clear through customs and have delivered to their premises. We will issue our own bill of lading.

Branching out, we can open offices in Phoenix, Salt Lake City and other points, either with our own people or using other companies as our agents, and publish through-tariff rates from those cities to Tokyo. Our agents in those cities will consolidate shipments and perhaps once a week send them to our Los Angeles CFS via truck.

We are operating what amounts to a steamship line without steamships! This permits you to ship on an FCA basis whether you are located in a seaport city or in an inland city.

And one more very important thing: An NVOCC can "advance" charges, such as cartage, inland freight and forwarding fees. So, by using an NVOCC service from a seaport or from an inland city, you can arrange to send the merchandise by truck "freight collect" to the CFS, and the NVOCC will pay the bill. You can arrange for the forwarder's bill to be sent to the NVOCC, and the NVOCC will pay the bill. The NVOCC will put these charges on their bills of lading as additional "collect" charges in addition to their own freight charges.

An NVOCC bill of lading might read:
Forwarding Advances: $175.00
Inland Freight Advances: $200.00
Ocean Freight: $300.00
Total Collect: $675.00

THE BEAUTY OF AN NVOCC

NVOCCs are very flexible in ways that steamship lines aren't. If you have a specific need, ask!

I once had a shipment suitable for a twenty-foot container. I moved it just as quickly (on the same vessel) and more economically with an NVOCC by loading it in the nose (front) of a forty-foot container. The NVOCC loaded the

rest of the container with other customers' freight going to the same port.

At destination, the other customers' freight was set aside for them. My shipment then cleared customs and rode on the container to my importer.

Where to Find NVOCCs

Many of the larger forwarders operate NVOCCs of their own. Many Customs Brokers act as inbound agents. There are also independents that you can locate in the *U.S. Custom House Guide* (see Resource List beginning on page 145).

NVOCCs generally operate in very heavy trade lanes with frequent sailings and enormous amounts of cargo moving. For the United States, this means to and from:
• Europe, especially Western Europe
• Australia and New Zealand
• Asia: Hong Kong, Japan, South Korea, Singapore, Taiwan

At some point, you may find yourself shipping FCA to Zurich, Switzerland, from an inland city, such as Phoenix, with all freight charges and the forwarder's bill going collect. I have done it many times, and it makes life so easy!

It's easy for the customer, too. A Zurich customer, for example, does not have to make his own arrangements to bring goods in from, say, the port of Rotterdam by truck or train. The goods arrive in Zurich, the customer clears customs and receives the goods.

If you import to Phoenix from Zurich, well, check NVOCCs with an eye to stipulating your routing in your letter of credit and using an economical routing all the way through. Publication 500 says that NVOCC bills of lading can only be used if the letter of credit specifically allows for them. Use this wording: "NVOCC Bills of Lading Acceptable." That's it!

AIR FREIGHT AND CONSOLIDATIONS

Traditionally, most air freight has moved either with the scheduled airlines (American Airlines, Trans World Airlines, etc.) or with airplanes owned or leased by a freight forwarder (Airborne Express, Emery Air Freight, etc.). Some very large shipments move via chartered planes.

In shipping via a scheduled airline, shipments might travel all or part of the way on a cargo aircraft or be on board an aircraft that carries both cargo and passengers. In the latter case a shipment is often "bumped" in favor of other priorities with the airline. Generally, the priority list is:

1. Fuel
2. Accompanied baggage
3. Unaccompanied baggage (sent on ahead)
4. Mail
5. Cargo

During the year-end holiday period, when planes are packed full of passengers (and baggage) and mail is at its height, cargo is frequently left behind.

Fortunately, an airline will date an air waybill with the *date of receipt ready for transportation*, not the on-board date. So as long as the shipment is delivered to the airline on a given date ready to be shipped, and with the air waybill in order, the airline will date it accordingly.

Remember, too, as we said in chapter seven, an air waybill (airline bill of lading) is *never negotiable*.

When a freight forwarder operates its own aircraft, "bumping" is unlikely, primarily because the aircraft do not carry passengers or baggage and may have limited mail contracts. However, these forwarder-operated aircraft do not necessarily operate to every point to which you may ship by air.

Many freight forwarders use *consolida-tion* service, similar to NVOCC service. The forwarder makes arrangements with airlines to handle a given number of air freight containers (smaller than ocean containers), or a given amount of weight, on a regular basis. As with the NVOCC, the freight forwarders are buying space wholesale and selling it retail. Also as with the NVOCC, the consolidations generally operate along very heavy cargo routes.

Consolidations to foreign cities may leave only once a week. However, it is still air freight, not ocean cargo, and freight shipped by air can often be available for customs clearance the day after shipment. If you time it right, a shipment can arrive very quickly after it is given to the forwarder. If you know that a consolidation to Frankfurt leaves your city every Tuesday night, and that the cargo is available in Frankfurt the next day, Tuesday morning is a logical time to deliver your air freight to the forwarder.

If you are in a smaller city, you may find that the forwarder will arrange to ship your cargo directly via airline to a "gateway" airport such as Atlanta, Chicago, Dallas, JFK (New York City) or Los Angeles, where there is enough cargo to fill weekly consolidations.

You may also find a possibility of making a domestic consolidation. Say you're in St. Louis. Your forwarder puts your cargo on his St. Louis-to-Dallas consolidation Tuesday morning with several domestic shipments. While the other shipments are being delivered in Texas, your cargo is loaded into a container for the Dallas-to-Frankfurt consolidation that night.

As your forwarder will "book" a container for your ocean shipment, air freight shipments can also be "booked" for advance reservations.

AIR CONSOLIDATIONS

With all our discussion about ocean ship-
ping, remember that most air forwarders can
arrange shipment by air consolidation, similar
in many ways to the ocean NVOCC.

A particular forwarder may have to contract
with an airline to move cargo from New York to
Frankfurt every Wednesday and Friday, and
from San Francisco to Tokyo every Tuesday and
Thursday. By moving your freight on these con-
solidations, you can often save significant air
freight dollars. (If you are near any city with an
airport, your forwarder can move your freight
on domestic flights to meet the consolidation.)

Some air freight forwarders compete avidly
for international freight by running their own
cargo jets to handle their consolidations.

SHIPPING VIA COD

Shipping via COD is relatively uncommon
in international trade, but it does exist for some
countries with some airlines and some for-
warders. COD is also generally available for
shipments to Canada by truck.

FOREIGN SALES CORPORATIONS

Foreign sales corporations were permitted
by Congress under legislation passed in
1984. They permit tax savings of as much
as 32 percent on income derived from export of goods manufactured or produced in
the United States.

A Foreign Sales Corporation is fairly
complicated to set up and maintain, requiring substantial legal and accounting assistance. It is definitely not something you
want to do on your own. Among other requirements, the Foreign Sales Corporation
must be incorporated "offshore," although
this can be the U.S. Virgin Islands or certain
other U.S. possessions. All stockholders'
meetings must be held outside the United

States. At least one member of the board of
directors must be a person who is not a
resident of the United States. A Foreign
Sales Corporation is incorporated as a company owned by a U.S. corporation.

Because of the cost and effort involved
in establishing and maintaining a Foreign
Sales Corporation, it is not something you
would ordinarily look at until you are approaching at least $500,000 in annual ex-
port sales. Then you can obtain preliminary
information from your tax accountant.

Shared Foreign Sales Corporations

A *shared Foreign Sales Corporation* is a way
to obtain some of the benefits of a foreign
sales corporation at a lower level of sales.
These Foreign Sales Corporations serve a
maximum of twenty-five exporters, all of
whom run their own businesses as usual,
taking advantage of the Foreign Sales Corporation benefits as a group. In your area,
these would be set up through state, county
or municipal governments, banks, or trade
groups.

COUNTERTRADE

Countertrade is usually outright barter and
can sometimes be easier for a small business
than it looks. Many countries do not have
enough dollars or other "hard" currencies
(British pounds, French francs, German
marks, Japanese yen, etc.) to buy what they
want. But they have products that people
here may want to buy.

Pepsico is doing this on a very large
scale. In exchange for syrup and technology
to make Pepsi products available in the
Commonwealth of Independent States (former USSR), Pepsico receives a steady supply of Stolichnaya vodka for resale in the
United States.

You may receive an offer for countertrade from a contact in Eastern Europe or a less-developed country in Africa or Asia. Explore these carefully and check out the company and the products as carefully as possible before committing yourself.

Most important, if you are trading your product for imported widgets, be sure of your costs (freight, duties, etc.) and be absolutely sure you have buyers for those widgets before you commit.

PROTECTIONS AND GUARANTEES

The following are important items to know about, even though your use for them may be limited.

Inspection

Sometimes you may want an import shipment inspected or tested before it is shipped to you. An organization that can arrange for everything from counting the shipment cartons to scientific tests is SGS (Société Generale de Surveillance). The U.S. member of the group is SGS International Quality Services, Division of U.S. Testing Company, Inc., 701 Lee Street, Des Plaines, IL 60016, (708) 296-8300, Fax: (708) 635-8414. They will be glad to quote you fees on any kind of inspection, anywhere, through their international affiliates.

In a letter of credit, you can specify that a certificate from that affiliate be presented to the bank certifying whatever you need: chemical content, voltage, English instruction manuals packed in each box.

The Export-Import Bank of the United States

The Export-Import Bank of the United States (ExIm Bank) is an agency of the United States government that arranges for guaranteed credit for export shipments. This can benefit you in two ways.

Sometimes a foreign buyer obtains credit guarantees for large purchases. (A few years ago, the Mexican petroleum company Pemex obtained multibillion dollar guarantees to purchase U.S. oil drilling equipment.) You would not apply for these guarantees directly, but you may find yourself negotiating with a large overseas buyer who already has a guarantee of payment for you.

The ExIm Bank can provide you with guarantees of payment on export shipments if you are concerned about the capability of the buyer, or even his bank, to pay.

You can purchase credit insurance directly from the ExIm Bank to guarantee payment. The insurance guarantees up to 95 percent of the commercial risks (bankruptcy, etc.) and up to 100 percent of the political risk (revolutions, etc.).

You can reach the ExIm Bank at (800) 565-3946. Be sure to ask about their New to Export program for companies that have been exporting for fewer than five years.

The Overseas Private Investment Corporation

Contact the Overseas Private Investment Corporation, Washington, DC 20527, for information on guarantees if you plan to invest overseas. This applies, for example, if you build a factory or even establish a branch office in a foreign country. This corporation is an agency of the U.S. government. They have direct loans available, also, for investment overseas.

CHAPTER ELEVEN

Planning Ahead for Import

- *The Importer's Outlay*

- *Basic Goals of U.S. Customs*

- *Understanding Tariffs*

- *Using the Harmonized Tariff Schedule*

- *Non-Duty Charges*

- *Customs Clearance*

Importing is the "other side of the transaction" from exporting. If you are importing, someone in a foreign country is exporting to you.

The terminology for the exporter is also the terminology for the importer. Where, as an exporter, you would quote EXW or CIF, now, as an importer, you are requesting quotes EXW or CIF. Instead of preparing a pro forma invoice, you prepare the order and receive a pro forma invoice in return. Instead of receiving the letter of credit, you open the letter of credit. It is up to you to spell out everything you need and to be sure that you are aware of the needs of the exporter (available ports, time required, etc.) in order to avoid amendments.

So we have already been through all the procedures, step by step, required to place an order, pay for it, and have the shipment moved to a U.S. port or airport. In this chapter we'll look at considerations specific to the importer.

PLAN FOR DOCUMENTATION

Before you order, make sure your documents are in order. Meet with your broker to discuss exactly what will be needed to clear Customs properly. Stipulate these documents in your letter of credit.

THE IMPORTER'S OUTLAY

As an exporter, you receive the order and letter of credit with the expectation that the importer has advised you of everything needed. You obtain an export license if needed, ship in accordance with the letter of credit and get paid. Once the shipment is gone and you have been paid, you are ready for the next order.

As an importer, when the shipment arrives you have spent your money and have a shipment of goods instead. You have to clear the shipment through customs, com-

plying with all laws, regulations and tariffs, and sell the product to recover your money and make a profit.

Remember that as an importer you have a number of costs to cover one way or another. Whether a shipment is EXW or CIF or anything in between, you are covering:

- The cost of goods
- Inland freight
- Forwarder's fees
- Loading charges
- Freight charges
- Insurance fees

And that is just to get it here. Once the goods are here, you also have:

- Customs duty
- Customs Broker's fees
- Inland freight to your warehouse

It is important to remember all these steps involve costs, and all of them are payable by you, the importer. You have to be able to cover them in your resale price and still make a profit!

So this brings in the following costs to be considered, *before* you place an order. (That does not mean before you start asking for catalogs from foreign countries but certainly before you do anything that commits you.)

- Storage (warehousing)
- Advertising
- Sales commissions
- Freight to the buyer's warehouse

Thousands of importers, large and small, do this every day. The key is planning. Do not bring a shipment into the port city and then find out what the duty is.

BASIC GOALS OF U.S. CUSTOMS

As we discussed in chapter three, U.S. Customs has two basic missions to carry out:

1. To protect the revenue due the United States of America. That is, to collect the appropriate amount of

duty on an import shipment.

2. To enforce all the other laws of the United States, the states, and the jurisdictions within the states (countries, cities, etc.).

The first mission is what we're concerned with in this section. (I'll discuss the second mission in chapter twelve.) U.S. Customs acts to collect the customs duty due on a shipment. The Customs Service, as part of the U.S. Treasury Department, takes its responsibility very seriously indeed. In fact, under federal law a person who has been discharged of his debts in bankruptcy court still is responsible for any customs duty or penalties he owed before he filed for bankruptcy.

GETTING THE BEST RATE

The savvy importer must consider two important questions:

1. *Are you getting the lowest possible duty rate? (Are your goods being classified properly? Is the rate for parts lower than the rate for an assembled unit? Maybe you should import the parts and do the assembly here.)*

2. *Can you get a lower rate by importing goods originating in a different country from your current source? Canadian and Mexican products have duty breaks under NAFTA that products made in other countries don't have.*

UNDERSTANDING TARIFFS

The key to actual customs duties (tariffs) is the Harmonized Tariff Schedule of the United States of America (HTSUSA). This book contains all the duty rates on all products from all countries. It is published by the U.S. government and is called "harmonized" because, since its adoption, its numbering system has been basically the same system as used by other industrialized

countries that have adopted the harmonized concept. The HTSUSA is also available as part of the *U.S. Custom House Guide*, which is privately published.

Both of these are listed in the Resource List and classification is discussed here. But I do not recommend that you buy them and try to classify import goods yourself. The reason is that although I use a simple example here, the system itself has many complications and "traps" for a person who is not familiar with it. There are lengthy classes about how to use the HTSUSA; if you are really interested in learning the system, please attend one of these classes. (Ask at a U.S. Customs office, a Customs Broker, or the international business professor at a local university. Most such classes are run by private organizations; these people would know about them.)

I will go through a classification now only as an example, to introduce you to the concepts, the vocabulary, and the general system (which, however, has plenty of exceptions). Your broker can serve you better if you are aware of what he or she needs to know to help you.

One important point to remember is this: You must discuss your plans with your broker before you place your order. Remember that your exporter cannot send you a pro forma invoice without knowing exactly what you need in terms of paperwork as well as product. It is always cheaper and easier to have everything ready in advance.

USING THE HARMONIZED TARIFF SCHEDULE

The HTSUSA, like the Schedule B, is based on a system of listing commodities in groups, from raw materials to the most advanced technical products.

For the following discussion, refer to the

HARMONIZED TARIFF SCHEDULE

HARMONIZED TARIFF SCHEDULE of the United States (1995)
Annotated for Statistical Reporting Purposes

Heading/ Subheading	Stat. Suf- fix	Article Description	Units of Quantity	Rates of Duty		
				1		2
				General	Special	
4901		Printed books, brochures, leaflets and similar printed matter, whether or not in single sheets:				
4901.10.00		In single sheets, whether or not folded.......	....	Free		Free
	20	Reproduction proofs......................	kg			
	40	Other.................................	kg			
		Other:				
4901.91.00		Dictionaries and encyclopedias, and serial installments thereof..............	....	Free		Free
	20	Dictionaries (including thesauruses)......................	No.			
	40	Encyclopedias.......................	No.			
4901.99.00		Other...........................	....	Free		Free
	10	Textbooks.........................	No.			
	20	Bound newspapers, journals and periodicals provided for in Legal Note 3 to this chapter..............	No.			
	30	Directories.......................	No.			
		Other:				
	40	Bibles, testaments, prayer books and other religious books........................	No.			
	50	Technical, scientific and professional books.............	No.			
		Art and pictorial books:				
	60	Valued under $5 each......	No.			
	65	Valued $5 or more each....	No.			
		Other:				
	70	Hardbound books..........	No.			
	75	Rack size paperbound books....................	No.			
		Other:				
	91	Containing not more than 4 pages each (excluding covers)..............	No.			
	92	Containing 5 or more pages each, but not more than 48 pages each (excluding covers)...	No.			
	93	Containing 49 or more pages each (excluding covers)...	No.			
4902		Newspapers, journals and periodicals, whether or not illustrated or containing advertising material:				
4902.10.00	00	Appearing at least four times a week..........	kg......	Free		Free
4902.90		Other:				
4902.90.10	00	Newspaper supplements printed by a gravure process........................	No......	1.6%	Free (A,CA,E,IL,J, MX)	25%
4902.90.20		Other.................................	....	Free		Free
	20	Newspapers appearing less than four times per week.................	kg			
	40	Other business and professional journals and periodicals (including single issues tied together for shipping purposes).....	No.			
	60	Other (including single issues tied together for shipping purposes)........................	No.			

excerpt on page 116. Heading 4901 is for "Printed books, brochures, leaflets and similar printed matter, whether or not in single sheets." Under that, there are subheadings for "In single sheets, whether or not folded" and "Other: Dictionaries and Encyclopedias."

Since the textbooks in the example are not in single sheets and are not considered to be dictionaries or encyclopedias, go to the next subheading of "Other" and you'll find "Textbooks" specifically listed.

Textbooks, bound newspapers and periodicals, Bibles, etc., are listed on specific lines for statistical purposes. When a customs entry is filed on the imported goods, the entire ten-digit number will be used. For textbooks, this is 4901.99.0010, but all the different goods that come under the "Other" subheading of 4901.99.00 have the same duty rate. In this case, good news: The goods come in duty free.

Similarly, items 4901.91.0020 (Dictionaries) and 4901.91.0040 (Encyclopedias) would be listed as different items on a customs entry, but both are rated according to heading 4901.91.00—again, duty free.

Why not lump all the duty-free items on the same page under one item number? There are three reasons:

1. The Harmonized System requires that the United States, along with all other countries that have adopted the system, be consistent with the first six numbers. Perhaps in some other countries, textbooks are duty free but dictionaries and encyclopedias are assessed duty.

2. Subheadings may change duty rates at some point, for whatever reason, so duty could thus be assessed against dictionaries and encyclopedias without affecting textbooks.

3. The classification numbers permit statistical record keeping by individual type of product.

In this instance, textbooks are easy to classify, because they are duty free in all instances. But what are the four columns following the article description all about? And notice, for item 4902.90.1000, newspapers printed by a gravure process, there are different rates listed in the different columns.

Units of Quantity

The first column, "Units of Quantity," is simply the way in which the quantity of the product imported will be listed on the customs entry. For textbooks, the Customs Service requests that you indicate the number ("No.") of textbooks you are bringing into the country. On the sample HTSUSA page, you will also see some items that must be shown by weight ("kg" for kilogram) and some items where no unit need be shown ("X"), similar to the Schedule B.

This is, again, usually for statistics. In some instances, duties are figured in whole or in part by the unit of quantity ($1 per each item imported, $1 per kilo, etc.).

Rates of Duty

Under "Rates of Duty" there are three separate categories. Column 1 is divided into "General" and "Special," and column 2 has no subdivisions.

Statutory Duty Rate

Let's start with column 2. This is what is known as the *statutory* rate of duty. Duty rates for all goods from all countries are assessed according to this column, except if otherwise provided. Actually, most countries are not in column 2 because of most-favored-nation treatment of other provisions.

For textbooks it does not matter. They are duty free in any case. But for newspapers "printed by a gravure process," the duty rate is 25 percent for a column 2 country.

Over the years, as efforts have succeeded to develop free trade and to lower duties worldwide, hardly any countries remain in column 2. They are the countries that are unfriendly to the United States and for whom special licenses are needed to trade with: Cuba, Iran, Iraq, Libya, North Korea, and others subject to federal law.

So, if you obtain a license to bring in newspaper supplements printed by a gravure process from any of these column 2 countries, the duty is 25 percent. Of course, textbooks, dictionaries and encyclopedias are free.

General Tariffs for Most Favored Nations

Column 1 indicates the rate for the countries that have most-favored-nation status. You have probably heard this phrase in the news, and here is fundamentally what it means.

At one time the United States set duty rates by country as well as by product. We gave lower tariff rates to certain countries for political reasons and because of long-standing trade relations. So a product coming in from Britain, a major U.S. trading partner and ally, might have been 1.8 percent, the lowest duty rate the U.S. had for that particular product. The same product coming in from other countries would have been higher, i.e., Britain would have been our most-favored-nation for that particular product. Likewise, our products would have enjoyed lower tariffs in Britain than the same products from other countries.

Over a period of time, treaties signed with other countries and the General Agreement on Tariffs and Trade (GATT) brought other countries into the most-favored-nation category. So, for example, goods in this classification from France and Germany were allowed in at the rate as applied to the same goods from our most-favored-nation—Britain.

Over time, other countries were added until now our rates of duty in column 1—General, the tariffs for our most favored nations among our trading partners, are now applicable to virtually all countries friendly to the United States. Indeed, since the founding of GATT after World War II, duty rates (tariffs) have been lowered worldwide on most imports. Under GATT the World Trade Organization will continue lowering trade barriers between nations.

So the rate of duty in column 1—General on item 4902.90.1000 is 1.8 percent, and is applicable to almost every U.S. trading partner.

Special Tariffs

So what is column 1—Special all about?

In addition to the statutory (column 2) and most-favored-nation (column 1—General) tariffs, there are special tariffs for certain commodities from certain countries due to specific treaties or agreements. Usually, they bring the duty even lower than the most-favored-nation rate.

Please note right from the beginning, if there is nothing in the Special column, then the General column applies to everyone with most-favored-nation status. The Special column lists just the exceptions—the "special" situations.

On the sample HTSUSA page, the only entries in column 1—Special are for the newspaper supplements printed by a gravure process, and they are as follows:

- (CA) Imports from Canada, under NAFTA and the earlier U.S.-Canadian Free Trade Agreement. Many items are now duty free or reduced duty, with the objective of wiping out all duties between the two countries by the end of the century.

- (MX) Imports from Mexico, under NAFTA. Many duties were eliminated on January 1, 1994, with all remaining duties scheduled to be phased out gradually. They are reduced each January 1 and different items will be duty free by January 1, 1999, 2004 or 2009.
- (A) This is also important. More than one hundred countries fall under this one category of exceptions, called the Generalized System of Preferences (GSP). Generally underdeveloped countries, the GSP countries enjoy duty reductions and sometimes (as here) duty-free treatment of goods that are otherwise dutiable. Federal law provides for this special tariff treatment in order to (1) increase trade and political linkages with these countries and (2) promote economic growth within these countries and increase prosperity among their peoples. Many different goods are included under the GSP provisions, but the provision applies only if an "A" or an "A*" is listed in the Special column for that particular classification. If neither is there, the GSP does not apply.
- (E) This is the Caribbean Basin Economic Recovery Act (CBERA), passed by the U.S. Congress and covering more than a dozen countries. One provision assists U.S. investors seeking to make investments in these countries. Another provision gives some imports from these countries lower duty or duty-free treatment by U.S. Customs. Like the General System of Preferences, a CBERA provision exists only if an "E" or "E*" is listed in the Special column for that particular classification. If neither of these is

listed there, CBERA does not apply.

- (J) This identifies treatment under the Andean Trade Preference Act. This provides for duty-free treatment for some items from Bolivia, Ecuador, Colombia and Peru.
- (IL) Imports from Israel, with whom the United States also has a Free Trade Agreement. Again, the special provisions only apply to the particular country and product if the appropriate letter is in the Special column for that exact classification.

CA and MX are the most important for importers in the United States, as part of the world's largest free trade agreement. For codes A, E and J, an important thing to consider is that many low-technology, labor-intensive products are included in these provisions, such as handmade baskets, rugs, etc. There are other products too, but these types of products are quite commonly included in both programs with our government's concept that money flows to the poorer people of the beneficiary country.

So if you are looking at these types of commodities, you may want to look closely at these programs. Current lists of the countries in each program are in both the HT-SUSA and the *U.S. Custom House Guide*.

Two other Special tariff provisions that you may run into are:

- (B), which covers goods under the Automotive Products Trade Act. This is special treatment for cars, trucks and some parts.
- (C), which is for the Agreement on Trade in Civil Aircraft. This covers imported helicopters, gliders and airplanes.

NON-DUTY CHARGES

Additional charges besides duty that are payable at the time of entry are:

- Merchandise Processing Fee. The Customs Service charges 0.19 percent (that's $^{19}/_{100}$ of 1 percent) as a fee for processing your merchandise into the country.
- Federal Excise Taxes. These apply to only a few imports, primarily alcoholic beverages. The Customs Service collects these taxes on behalf of the federal government.
- Harbor Maintenance Fee. On ocean imports, a fee of 0.125 percent is payable (that's $^1/_8$ of 1 percent) (see Export Vessel Movement Summary Sheet explanation on page 90). For importers this fee is collected at the time of entry.

CUSTOMS CLEARANCE

Clearing goods through U.S. Customs is not just a matter of going down to the Customhouse, identifying your shipment and paying the duty. It can be a simple process for smaller shipments, an extremely complex process for larger shipments. U.S. Customs differentiates between "small" and "large" based on the value of the shipment.

The types of entries discussed below are called consumption entries—the goods are being cleared through U.S. Customs to be sold or otherwise consumed in the United States.

Informal Entry

Informal entry covers most imports valued at $1,249.99 and under, if not included under quota or a few other exceptions. (See chapter twelve for quota information.) This is simply an abbreviated Customs clearance procedure for shipments of small value.

An informal entry is the easiest. I suggest that you retain a licensed Customs Broker to arrange Customs clearance for you, but it is possible to do it yourself. Let's say you plan to clear the shipment yourself. You will check with the steamship line or airline to determine when the shipment will be available for clearance. The carrier and U.S. Customs can advise you how to arrange for an inspector to be available for Customs clearance at an approximate time.

This procedure differs from one port city to another. In some ports, Customs inspectors start at given points and rotate among the carriers until the day's shipments are cleared. One inspector may go from airline A to B to C to D; another may go from airline E to F to G to H. If your shipment is at airline D or H, you may have to wait the entire morning or afternoon for the inspector to reach you.

The Customs Brokers will have messengers or "runners" accompanying the inspectors from carrier to carrier, because they will probably have at least one shipment for one of their customers at each carrier on a given day.

The documents you will need are the carrier's bill of lading, invoices and packing slips. In some cases you will need other documents (see below under "Formal Entry"). It saves everyone time if you already have an idea of the tariff classification at this point.

When your shipment is ready to be cleared, the inspector will ask you to open it for inspection. He will verify that the goods inside the packaging conform to the descriptions on the paperwork, that the value shown appears to be accurate, and that the goods are properly marked with the country of origin. He will assist you in preparing the informal entry documentation, figuring the duty, if any, and collecting the duty payment from you.

At that point, he will stamp the paperwork "Cleared U.S. Customs" and, after paying any freight or other charges due the carrier, the shipment is yours to take with you or to have delivered for you.

At the time the shipment is cleared, it is considered liquidated. What this means is that the paperwork you and the inspector have completed is not subject to further audit by the Customs Service. With few exceptions, neither the Customs Service nor you can question the classification, duty or arithmetic ever again.

KEEPING YOUR BROKER INFORMED

Before you import anything, your broker needs to know the following:

1. *What are you importing?*
   a) *What is it called?*
   b) *What is it made of?*
   c) *What is it used for?*
   d) *How is it packed (assembled, unassembled)?*
2. *What is the country of origin?*
3. *What is the value?*
4. *How will it be coming in (air, ocean, mail)?*

GOOD NEWS FOR SHIPMENTS OF LESS THAN $200

An abbreviated procedure for shipments of less than $200, established in 1994, permits the carrier to file entry for the import without need for Customs Service classification or payment of duty.

This procedure is primarily meant for clearing samples and one-time small-value imports. It was initiated at the request of many small package couriers.

Customs clearance on these shipments will be undertaken by the carrier.

Formal Entry

Formal entry applies to shipments $1,250 or more in value and all shipments under

quota. A formal entry must be cleared by a licensed Customs Broker in virtually all instances. Here is why.

A formal entry is not liquidated ("closed") until the Customs Service has had an opportunity to audit the documents submitted. This can be a year or later after the actual date of entry at the Customhouse. At the time of liquidation, Customs can bill you for additional duty, refund overpayment, or otherwise correct or require correction of any discrepancy it finds. In fact, the money paid as duty under a formal entry is actually called "Deposit of Estimated Duties."

You must post a bond with the Customs Service to guarantee payment of any additional monies owed. A bonding company will not sell you a bond unless the entry is being taken care of by a licensed Customs Broker. By your use of a Customs Broker, the bonding company has confidence that the paperwork will be prepared as accurately as possible.

There are some exceptions. You can, for example, post a cash bond with the Customs Service, but this is usually impractical for the average importer. Some very large importers obtain bonds because they have their own import departments, often with licensed Custom Brokers in charge. For all practical purposes though, for a formal entry you need a bond, and to get a bond you need a licensed Customs Broker.

Also, the paperwork for a formal entry is much more involved than for an informal entry. U.S. Customs will not provide the assistance that they will in preparing an informal entry.

In many cases, a Customs Broker can transmit entry documentation via computer (Automated Broker Interface, or ABI) even before your shipment arrives in the port. The broker will need the following:

- Carrier's bill of lading

- Invoices
- Packing slips
- Power of attorney—required before a Customs Broker can act on your behalf (the broker will have the form)
- Your IRS number (Social Security number or, for a corporation, Employer Identification Number)

The Customs Broker can arrange for customs entry and clearance of your shipment and delivery to your location. You will receive an itemized statement from the broker for all services rendered.

If you wish, as the importer of record, you can make out one check to U.S. Customs for the estimated duty and a separate check to the broker for his charges.

Many importers prefer the broker to call after the shipment has cleared. At that time, you can make the decision to pick up the goods yourself or have them delivered to your warehouse.

Mail Entry

Shipments entering the United States by mail can be expedited if they are $1,249.99 or less in value and are not under quota or other restrictions.

For a mail shipment to be accepted under the expedited procedure, a Customs declaration must be affixed to the outside of the package by the exporter in the foreign country. (See chapter eight for samples of U.S. forms for U.S. exporters.)

It is preferable for an invoice and a packing slip to be in an envelope attached to the outside of the package. This way if a Customs Service employee needs it, it is easy to find. You should instruct your exporter on both of these points.

A Customs inspector will do the informal entry for the shipment, including figuring the duty, and release the package to be delivered by the U.S. Postal Service. At the

time of delivery, the letter carrier will request payment of duty from the importer.

If a shipment is $1,250 or more, or if it is under quota or other restrictions, a formal entry is required. The package will be held at the post office nearest the Customhouse, and a card will be sent to you by mail requesting that you make arrangements for Customs clearance. Keep the card for your Customs Broker—it has a reference number on it that identifies the location of your package at the post office, perhaps among thousands.

Your exporter should supply the same documentation as for other mail shipments:

- Customs declaration
- Invoice
- Packing slip

All of this should be on the *outside* of the package. It saves you time and expense if you ask your exporter to fax you a copy of both the invoice and the packing slip on the day of mailing. Give these to your Customs Broker with the postcard, and he can prepare the Customs paperwork in advance of the trip to the post office.

Air Shipment Entry

One reason why air waybills are not negotiable under a letter of credit is the shipment usually gets to the destination before the documents get through the banking system.

Ask your Customs Broker what documentation you'll need to clear an air shipment when it arrives. This will be at least an invoice and a packing slip. Advise your vendor to attach copies of these documents, in an envelope, to the *outside* of one of the cartons in your shipment.

DOCUMENTATION FOR THE AIR IMPORTER

Because your shipment will move faster than banking documents, stipulate that a copy of each and every document (photocopies acceptable) should be:

1. *In an envelope taped to the outside of one of the cartons of your shipment.*
2. *In an envelope attached to the air waybill (as a backup set).*

Value of the Shipment

Customs generally accepts the "Transaction Value" as shown on the invoice as being the value of the merchandise for purposes of figuring duty. Transaction value is defined as the "price actually paid or payable when sold for exportation to the United States."

"The price actually paid" if you prepaid or paid under a letter of credit or sight draft.

"Payable" if you bought on open account.

"For exportation to the United States" on the pier or at the airport, ready to go. This means FAS value (see chapter five).

The following costs are not dutiable:

- Ocean or air freight, truck or rail freight
- Forwarder's fees
- Insurance fees

So if you bought CFR or CIF, you are entitled to determine the amount of these costs and deduct them from your invoice before figuring duty.

Although most of the shipments the average importer brings in are figured on transaction value, there are some exceptions, based primarily on the following: (1) if there is a restriction on the use of the goods; (2) related parties (you are buying literally, from a relative, or from a subsidiary or other affiliate of your company). Please be aware that there are some exceptions, and your Customs Broker will tell you in advance if any apply. (Of course, you talk with your broker well in advance.)

Complying With the U.S. Customs Service

The U.S. Customs Service is a very old and powerful agency. If you look at the U.S. Customs insignia, you will note that there are only eleven stars on the emblem instead of the thirteen you might expect. This is because U.S. Customs was in operation before the last two states had ratified the Constitution. So they have been examining shipments and paperwork since before the first thirteen colonies were part of the United States.

Honesty and Accuracy

Sometimes people are tempted to try to "bend the law" in their favor or even tamper with documents in order to pay less duty or to have an informal shipment instead of a formal shipment. This is fraud, a felony punishable by heavy fines and sentencing to a federal prison. The Customs Service has been catching people at it since 1789.

I caution you in the strongest possible terms to be totally accurate and honest in your dealings with the Customs Service at all times.

Will My Shipment Be Inspected?

Because of the growth of international trade, U.S. Customs no longer inspects every shipment. The Customs Service targets shipments for inspection based on a variety of criteria, such as the exporter, country of exporter, importer, type of commodity, etc. In other words, they concentrate on inspecting shipments based on past experience. However, they also constantly spot-check shipments from all destinations. If anyone ever tells you "Customs never inspects shipments from country X," don't believe it.

Meeting Customs Laws and Regulations

- *Making Use of Special Entries*

- *Importing Within the Law*

- *Quotas*

- *Keep It in Perspective*

In the last chapter we looked at the role of U.S. Customs as it applies to the Harmonized Tariff Schedule and consumption entries (informal and formal). But the role of the Customs Service extends beyond duty rates and ordinary entries. In this chapter we'll examine some special types of entries, the laws and regulations the Customs Service is charged with enforcing and import quota shipments.

MAKING USE OF SPECIAL ENTRIES

A number of special types of Customs entries may benefit you, depending on the importing situation.

In-Transit Entry

If you are located in an inland city and are importing by ocean carrier, you may use in-transit (IT) entries quite often.

Let's say that you are in Nogales, Arizona, which is a border crossing and a U.S. Customs-designated port of entry, but not a seaport. A shipment is coming in via a West Coast or Gulf Coast port: Los Angeles or Long Beach, Houston or Galveston. You have two choices in arranging Customs clearance:

1. You may arrange Customs clearance at the port city and then have the goods moved by truck or rail to Nogales.
2. You may arrange for an IT to be written at the port city and presented to the Customs Service, assigning a specific reference number to your shipment. It will then move to Nogales by a Customs Service-approved truck or rail carrier under Customs bond. At Nogales, you will arrange Customs clearance as usual with a consumption entry. When the Consumption

Entry is filed, the IT reference number is shown on it. At that point, the IT entry is liquidated.

By arranging for an IT at the port, you can clear customs in your city, or in the Customs port city nearest you. If there are any difficulties, or if any clarification is needed, you will find it much easier to work with both the Customs Broker and the Customs Service.

Warehouse Entry

A *warehouse entry* is just what it sounds like: The goods are going into a warehouse. Why? Because if you store goods in a Customs-approved bonded warehouse, you don't have to pay duty until the goods are taken out of the warehouse. Perhaps your buyer is not ready for the goods yet. You have to store the goods anyway, and this way you postpone paying the duty.

Perhaps the goods have a very high duty rate, and you want to pull them out (and pay the duty) as you run low on stock. The important thing is that duty is postponed until the goods are removed. How long? Up to five years under present law. Also, IRS excise taxes, such as those on liquor, are postponed until the goods are taken out of the bonded warehouse. And during this time, you can repack the goods, clean, sort and undertake other activities as long as they do not amount to a manufacturing process, which is not allowed in a bonded warehouse.

When goods are removed from a bonded warehouse, a *warehouse withdrawal* is filed with the Customs Service and duty is paid.

Foreign Trade Zones

Foreign trade zones require special attention as "super bonded warehouses." Although not as common as bonded warehouses, there are nonetheless more than a hundred around the country.

The major difference is that manufacturing and display are permitted in the foreign trade zone, or FTZ. Some companies retain space in FTZ on a regular basis for assembly or to show samples and prototypes of new goods to their customers. Goods can also be sold from within an FTZ. Each customer files a consumption entry when the goods are being withdrawn.

An important note about FTZs: Treatment by the Customs Service can change when the goods change inside the zone. For instance, if you brought in all automotive parts and shipped out only finished cars, Customs considers that you are entering finished cars on your consumption entry, and duty is payable at that rate.

Temporary Import Under Bond

Temporary import under bond (TIB) applies to goods brought into the United States for special purposes, then exported again. TIB is most commonly used for trade show, sales and other exhibition materials, and for goods brought into the United States for repair, but it also applies to such items as racing cars brought in for a specific race.

When goods are imported as a TIB, a bond is posted to guarantee their export. At the time of export, paperwork is done with Customs Service to match the export with the TIB.

Also keep TIB in mind if you are exporting something that will be brought back to the United States, since many other countries also have TIB procedures.

Carnet Imports

A carnet is one step beyond TIB. It is more or less a passport for the goods. Similar to your passport, subject to inspection and visa stamps when entering and leaving foreign countries, a carnet covers goods that will be entering and leaving several different countries before making the return to their country of origin.

American Goods Returned Imports

American goods returned (AGR) imports are entered like other goods but are always duty free. If you purchase goods from a foreign country that are actually made in the United States, or if goods made in the United States are returned for repair or from a consignment shipment, they enter the United States duty free.

But beware: U.S.-made trademarked goods sold in foreign countries are sometimes imported into the United States by people anxious to turn a quick profit. This is called the "gray market." It is not exactly the black market, but if you are importing trademarked goods for resale without the permission of the rightful owner of the trademark, you can find yourself in some trouble with the Customs Service, and in a civil lawsuit from the trademark owner, too. This goes double for patented products.

IMPORTING WITHIN THE LAW

In chapter eleven I defined the mission of U.S. Customs as being twofold:

1. To protect the revenue due the United States.
2. To enforce all the other laws of the United States, the states, and the jurisdictions within the states.

In this section we will explore the second mission—the laws U.S. Customs is responsible for enforcing.

CUSTOMS ENFORCES ALL LAWS

In its role of enforcing the law, U.S. Customs enforces state and local laws. Suppose you were an importer of liquor, and you imported a shipment through a port in a dry county where alcohol was illegal by local ordinance. The Customs Service would not release the goods to you unless you could show that the goods were to be transported out of the county and to be sold for consumption.

Prohibited Articles

Certain articles cannot be brought into the United States at all:

- Counterfeit articles
- Obscene, immoral or seditious material
- Products of convicts or forced labor
- Endangered species of birds and animals, including their skin, tusks, feathers and fur, and products made from them
- Lottery tickets
- White or yellow phosphorous matches
- Switchblade knives

If you are considering importing any of these products, think again. You would be operating outside the law and would be subject to harsh punishment.

Intellectual Property Laws

Intellectual property refers to something that is patented, trademarked or copyrighted. If someone else holds these rights to a product, you may not import it. You would be just as guilty of violating the law as if you manufactured that item in your own city. If you hold the patent, trademark or copyright, then of course you are protected by the same laws. U.S. Customs procedures allow information about these intellectual property rights to be recorded so they can be protected at the various ports.

Licensing

In chapter one I posed the question, "Do you need a license to import goods into the United States?" I discussed that briefly in terms of some countries considered unfriendly to the United States. But, beyond that, certain industries have licensing requirements. The general rule is that if you need a license to manufacture, buy or sell the item, you need a license to import it.

For example, it is perfectly legal to import penicillin into the United States. It is a legal drug used for beneficial purposes. However, U.S. Customs will not release the shipment to you unless you have the appropriate pharmaceutical license for your state, thus enforcing your state's laws as well as federal drug laws.

On the other hand, while heroin and cocaine are generally illegal to import, special licenses are issued for them to properly licensed pharmaceutical companies that use them to manufacture powerful prescription drugs.

Other major types of goods that cannot be imported into the United States by anyone except those holding the appropriate licenses required in that industry are:

- Alcohol
- Firearms, including ammunition
- Radioactive materials
- Radiation-producing products (X-ray equipment, etc.)

Other Product Regulations

Certain products must comply with laws that are administered by a variety of United States agencies. For example, the Food and Drug Administration has laws to help protect the purity of foods sold in the United States. Since you have to comply with those laws to manufacture food in the United States, you also have to comply with those laws to import food into the United States.

When an imported product is subject to laws administered by other United States agencies (the FDA, for example), U.S. Customs asks those agencies for clearance. Here is a list of some of the products and government agencies involved:

- *Any edible product, whether to be consumed by humans or animals.* Sometimes the product is tested by the Food and Drug Administration, sometimes by the Department of Agriculture.
- *Anything alive, including livestock, domestic animals, wild animals, poultry, insects, plants and bacteria.* Department of Agriculture; Food and Drug Administration; U.S. Fish and Wildlife Service.
- *Some plant products, including seeds.* Department of Agriculture; Food and Drug Administration.
- *Radios, televisions, VCRs, computers, etc., that produce radiation or require licenses.* Federal Communications Commission.
- *Household appliances.* Department of Energy; Federal Trade Commission.
- *Cosmetics.* Food and Drug Administration.
- *Gold and silver.* Department of Justice ensures that purity is accurately indicated.
- *Pesticides.* Environmental Protection Agency.
- *Hazardous materials.* Department of Transportation.
- *Textile products, wool and wool products, fur and fur products.* Federal Trade Commission—accuracy in labeling.
- *General consumer products.* Consumer Products Safety Commission.

THE MANY LAWS TO CONSIDER

An importer is both subject to and protected by a wide range of laws. In all your dealings, you must operate within laws stipulated by the following:

- *United States Constitution*
- *Treaties to which the United States is a party*
- *United States statutes*
- *Executive orders (issued by the President)*
- Customs Regulations of the United States of America
- *Harmonized Tariff Schedule of the United States of America*
- *Regulations of federal agencies other than the Customs Service*
- *State constitutions*
- *State statutes*
- *State regulations*
- *City, county and other local statutes and regulations*

Marking and Labeling

Marking and labeling constitute an extremely important area, one in which importers sometimes get into trouble simply because they did not tell the exporter what was needed.

Essentially, all products imported into the United States must be labeled clearly with the country of manufacture, unless the product is specifically exempted in the *Customs Regulations of the United States.* Exempted products range from works of arts to Christmas trees to wire (except barbed wire). Anything not exempted that is imported into the country must be marked in such a way that the ultimate purchaser can determine the country of origin.

For example: If you import shirts packed twenty-four to the carton, and the outside of the carton is marked "Made in Malaysia," the shirts themselves still have to be marked because the ultimate purchaser—the consumer—does not buy shirts in quantities of twenty-four of the same size, color and style.

Shirts ordinarily are marked on a label inside the collar. Whether the shirts are displayed for sale folded or on a hanger, the country of origin is visible to the ultimate purchaser.

Various types of merchandise have special marking requirements. Some of these requirements are U.S. law, some are U.S. Customs regulations, and some are other agencies' regulations that are enforced by U.S. Customs.

These are only a few examples:

- Clock movements working on jewels must be clearly marked to show the number of jewels.
- Gold and silver ingots or bars must be clearly marked to show their purity (14-karat gold, sterling silver, etc.).
- Dishwashers, refrigerators and many other appliances must be clearly marked to show their annual energy expenditure.
- Hazardous substances must be clearly marked as to proper handling and disposal.
- Textile products must be clearly marked with fiber content information (percentages of cotton, wool, polyester, etc.).

Import What You Know

This may all sound very complex, and it would be if you were a conglomerate importing all these different types of goods. You may never import anything subject to specific licensing or special requirements. If, however, you are interested in importing one or another of these types of products, the odds are great that you are already in that business. If you are, then you are already familiar with the licensing, inspections, labeling, etc., for your particular industry.

If you are not yet involved in a business that requires special licensing and you want to import, I advise you as strongly as possible to get involved with the industry first and learn its ins and outs before attempting to do so as an importer. This will save you a great deal of expense and trouble. And again, speak to your Customs Broker before you begin importing.

QUOTAS

I alluded briefly to quotas in chapter eleven, saying that quota shipments can never be brought in under informal entry. As many countries do, the United States has quotas to regulate the quantities of some products that are permitted to enter the country. This is usually done to protect domestic industries.

Here is a partial list of the types of products that are under quotas:

- Animal feeds
- Candies
- Chocolates
- Cotton
- Dairy products
- Peanuts (but not peanut butter)
- Sugar
- Textile products

Some of these, again, are quotas imposed under U.S. Customs law or regulation. Others, such as some of the quotas for dairy products, are in accordance with other laws or regulations (Department of Agriculture for many of the dairy quotas). The Customs Service acts to enforce all quotas.

In the United States there are two types of quotas:

1. Absolute Quota—Only so much of the product can be brought in during a year, or other period of time.
2. Tariff-Rate Quota—So much of the product can be brought in during a year at a given duty rate; a higher rate is then imposed upon additional goods brought in.

In some instances, where absolute quotas fill gradually during the quota period (calendar year, for example), the Customs Service clears shipments of incoming merchandise until the quota is finally reached and then denies clearance to additional shipments. The Customs Service will inform you at any point where the quota stands.

In other cases, when the quota is expected to fill immediately or very quickly, all entries are to be submitted in their respective ports so as to be accepted at noon Eastern Time the day the quota opens. If the quota is exceeded, each importer is given a percentage that can be brought in under a consumption entry.

With a tariff-rate quota, goods are simply imported until the quota is reached, and then the duty rate is increased on succeeding imports.

If you import goods after a quota is closed, you can place them in a bonded warehouse or a foreign trade zone until the quota reopens, and then file a consumption entry. This, however, means storage charges, Customs Brokers' fees and delayed sales. Also, some goods can spoil, or in the case of textiles, go out of style.

STAYING ABREAST OF CHANGING REGULATIONS

Shortly after the passage of NAFTA, a new importer came into a broker's office complaining that the Customs Service wouldn't release his import from Mexico. He needed a formal entry. The merchandise was under quota. It was dutiable.

He thought all merchandise from Mexico was simply duty free and all he had to do was bring it in! *(And this was in December, 1993. NAFTA had been passed, but was not yet implemented.)*

Laws and regulations affecting international trade are many and complex and changing all the time. Keep your forwarder and/or broker advised of your plans for a new shipment. Before *it moves.*

KEEP IT IN PERSPECTIVE

Import may seem extremely complicated, but it is really as complicated or uncomplicated as the businesses and industries themselves.

For example, if you are in the business of dealing with gold and silver ingots, and you already have experience in the field, the requirements for marking ingots with the purity of the metal are probably something you already know by heart. The regulations simply extend to importing the goods as well as selling them domestically.

If you are in the textile business, the proper labeling of fabric content is quite familiar to you. Quotas would be something new.

No matter how much importing you do, you are probably going to be involved in what amounts to only a few pages in the Harmonized Tariff Schedule and the *Customs Regulations.*

Overall, you are subject to obeying the law of the land just as you are now. Lawyers will tell you that a court considers "everyone is presumed to know the law." So the important thing is, with the help of your broker, to research the laws and regulations that affect your proposed shipment—before you do it—and remain well within the spirit as well as the letter of the law.

The Risks and Rewards of International Trade

As we have discussed, there are risks involved in international trade as there are in any area of business. And to the degree possible, through letters of credit and using expert assistance, you can minimize the risk. However, be aware that the risk is still there.

In this chapter we'll look at some pitfalls to be wary of, explore some ideas for turning potential hazards into positive experiences, and examine some of the foreign markets that are ready and waiting for you.

FRAUD

In the domestic mail-order business, there are many legitimate companies with which you can place an order by check or credit and expect prompt delivery of your merchandise. Most offer money-back guarantees. But many fly-by-night companies have no intention to ship anything: All they want is your check, or better yet, your credit card number. Likewise, there are indeed people around the world who attempt to defraud.

The best person to protect you from any possible financial loss is your banker. If you have any doubt at all about the validity of a financial document, it should be brought to your banker's attention immediately. Ideally, the documents are being negotiated through your local international banker anyway.

I once received the largest order for a particular product in the history of my company. I also had in hand the largest bad check in the history of my company—for more than $100,000. Actually it was a draft, which we received by airmail from Nigeria. With the draft was a letter placing an order for a "product mix which in your experience would be best for our market."

Personally, I won't go into a donut shop for a dozen donuts without picking out the particular ones I want. I certainly would not leave it up to a manufacturer to send me a $100,000 shipment made up "as he thought best."

That was the first tip-off that something was wrong. Second, the draft was sent to us by mail direct from the prospective importer. We ship the goods (air freight prepaid) and send a letter with the draft, directly to his bank, certifying that the goods were sent.

Now a draft ordinarily would have originated with the exporter (me). A letter of credit would have originated not with him but with his bank. So a draft coming directly from him was immediately suspect.

I sent a copy of the correspondence to our local international banker and asked that he check it out. The word came back the next day: No such bank in Nigeria.

So their scam was to try to get a U.S. company to ship the goods air freight (which means directly consigned, not to order), prepaid (even getting the shipper to pay the freight for them!) for $100,000 worth of goods and then have the draft bounce off a nonexistent bank.

Actually our local bank would have learned it was nonexistent when first trying to put the draft through. But if we had done what these folks wanted us to do, they would have had the goods before we knew something was wrong. Then they could close down and reopen at a new address under a new name.

And isn't it possible that they sent out hundreds—even thousands—of letters and would be happy to receive just one shipment from one innocent victim?

I am telling you this story not to try to scare you off, but only to remind you to exercise normal business prudence. If a U.S. company you had never heard of presented you with a check for $100,000, asking you to send a shipment (of whatever product mix you thought best), truck freight prepaid, wouldn't you call first and at least see if the check was good?

Exercise normal caution. If something doesn't look right, check it out thoroughly

STEERING CLEAR OF BOYCOTTS

Under U.S. law and regulations, it is illegal for a U.S. firm to participate in boycotts of shipments to foreign countries with whom the United States enjoys friendly relations. It is also illegal for you to *state* to anyone that you are participating in a boycott, whether you are actually participating in it or not.

Sooner or later, you will receive a request from a potential foreign vendor asking you to certify that you are a party to a boycott. (This may not happen until letter of credit time!) When it does come up, I caution you in the strongest possible terms to refuse to do any such certification and to refuse to participate actively in a boycott, even if it means losing the sale. This can keep you out of serious trouble.

If you are requested to participate in a boycott, or to certify that you are doing so, the request itself must be reported to the U.S. Department of Commerce.

Such situations most frequently occur when certain importers in certain Middle East countries ask a U.S. firm to certify that it is boycotting sales to Israel.

BRIBERY

Much of what constitutes routine business in some parts of the world is considered bribery in the United States—cash payments or "gifts" to a public official in exchange for government approval or permits, or even a visa or U.S. Customs clearance. If you make a payment that could be considered a bribe under U.S. law, you can be prosecuted under

U.S. law, in accordance with the Foreign Corrupt Practices Act.

If someone solicits you for what you consider to be a bribe, or if you feel that "voluntarily" offering a bribe would smooth things along, do not get involved. It can lead to a great deal of trouble for you. It is even possible that you are being set up by someone who will turn you in to authorities in the foreign country as well.

As long as you limit your foreign business endeavors to exporting from the United States and importing into the United States, you should be distant enough from any such offers anyway. They come up more often when a U.S. company is opening a branch overseas, or a factory, or is itself involved in customs clearance abroad. If you let your foreign business partner deal with his government, such situations should rarely come up.

DO I NEED AN EXPORT LICENSE?

Chapter one briefly discussed export licensing, and chapter twelve discussed import licensing in detail. You may never need to obtain a validated export license. But if you deal with commodities that do require a validated license, for any reason, you are responsible for obtaining the license. And you can get into a great deal of trouble exporting goods without one.

The basic concept behind export licenses is as follows.

You have an inherent license to export general commodities to most countries. Even though you do not have a piece of paper in your wallet or on your wall certifying that you are permitted to export from the United States, you nonetheless have a license as real as a driver's license. This license is granted to you by operation of law. If you violate export laws and regulations, this license, your "permission to export," can be taken away from you.

You need a validated export license, an actual piece of paper issued by the United States government, to export certain goods to certain countries. The major categories, as outlined earlier, are: (1) weapons, (2) high-tech items, and (3) commodities in short supply.

Sometimes items you may not expect to need licensing require it: (certain) blueprints, household electronic or office computer equipment, watercraft, and endangered fish and wildlife.

Since you will probably deal in just a few types of commodities, you can determine if you need any validated licenses relatively easily. Check with the U.S. Department of Commerce. If you don't need validated licenses, exporting is especially easy for you. If you do need a validated license, the Department of Commerce will assist you in the license application procedure. Ask for a copy of their free booklet, "Summary of Export Controls," as a good background on the subject.

MAKING THE MOST OF YOUR TRIPS ABROAD

If you maintain your business presence within the United States, it may be quite some time before you travel abroad. Your visit will probably be one of two possible types: to a trade show as an exhibitor or a visitor, or to foreign companies as a prospective buyer or seller.

Foreign travel is extremely fascinating. I find it most enjoyable to "do as the Romans do" and, certainly in industrialized countries, stay in indigenous hotels and eat in restaurants featuring the local cuisine. In the United States I can stay at the Hyatt and enjoy McDonald's anytime.

Here are my tips for enjoying the trip to the fullest and staying out of trouble. Keep your passport and visa with you at all times and keep photocopies of both in your luggage. In some jurisdictions the local police routinely confiscate your passport temporarily to run a background check to determine if you are an undesirable alien. In that case, keep the photocopies with you, on your person.

Keep the telephone number and address of the local United States consulate with you. In case of difficulties, consulate officials can help you obtain medical or legal assistance, emergency funds from back home, even a duplicate passport. If you go somewhere "off the beaten path," advise the local consulate of where you are going, where you can be reached, and when you expect to return. If you are overdue, they will contact the local police authorities.

In case of demonstrations or other disturbances, *go somewhere else*. Watch it on the news that night instead.

I have talked a great deal about the cultural gaps and the fact that you can get along in international trade quite well knowing only English. Of course, it is always better to know a little of your foreign business partner's language, and it is important to provide an interpreter if your partner is uncomfortable in English. But when visiting another country, it is much more important to know at least a few phrases and to understand something of the cultural dos and don'ts. You can put your foot in your mouth, so to speak, much more easily in person than over the phone.

If you have time, take a class at a community college or language school. You will have a chance to speak, read, write and listen to the language, and the teachers go out of their way to introduce you to the cultural patterns as well as the history. Usually they will spend some time discussing gestures that may have quite different meanings in the country you visit. Knowing something about the history of the country adds tremendously to your own enjoyment of the trip, too.

If you don't have time to take a class, or don't consider yourself enough of a linguist, stop at the local library and borrow a taped lesson in the basics of the language. You will be amazed how much you can learn in a short period of time. Or ask someone who already knows the language to coach you in some phrases that you think you will find useful. Your foreign business partner will respect you very highly for your efforts.

MAINTAINING CREDIBILITY

I started this chapter talking about some of the charlatans you can meet in international trade. To establish a long-term business relationship with honest business partners abroad you must maintain the highest possible standards in your own business undertakings. This means that you:

- Stand behind your quotations (pro forma invoices).
- Stick to your promised shipping dates.
- Extend discounts as promised.
- Provide backup (sales literature, training) as promised, when promised.
- Answer all correspondence promptly and in full detail.

Maintaining your high standards also includes treating your foreign customer—or the foreign inquiry whom you hope will become a customer—with the respect and courtesy you feel you would deserve in return. A foreign partner who has been in business long enough has probably been stung, either by people in his or her own country or in international dealings or both. Probably you have, too.

Good business people are always anxious to be part of an honest transaction and are always wary of the person who may try to take advantage of their honesty. Therefore, while you are being careful, recognize that the other person is being careful, too. Don't give a potential customer or vendor reasons to doubt your sincerity and find someone else. Keep your credibility and you will establish a relationship that will last for many mutually profitable years to come.

QUALITY STANDARDS AND ISO 9000

The International Standards Organization (ISO) in Geneva, Switzerland, has established guidelines for quality assurance systems in companies. One or another potential customer may ask for ISO 9000 certification from you (and then again they may not).

Entire books are written on the subject, and certification is an involved procedure. (If you are acting as a middle agent, you can inquire about the ISO 9000 status from the actual manufacturer.) Information on ISO 9000 is available from: Standards, Code and Information Program, National Institute of Standards and Technology, Building 101, Room A629, Gaithersburg, MD 20899.

AVOID NAMING ANYONE YOUR "AGENT"

In establishing a solid international business relationship, you will have customers, dealers, distributors, perhaps even a distributor to whom you have given an exclusive arrangement for their countries. Normally, they will all buy products from you and resell the products in their countries.

Regardless of your business relationship, be wary of naming anyone your "agent." Giving someone that title may seem innocent, but an agent can make commitments on your behalf. A reference to "our agent" in a fax can result in serious consequences when the "agent" does something down the road. For example, an "agent" who commits you to a specific delivery schedule or to purchase goods for your eventual import, and does so without your knowledge, may be able to actually bind you to that agreement.

The next time you visit your lawyer's office, ask him to show you the shelves of books in the law library—all to unravel the very complicated law of "principal and agent." You can avoid this simply by avoiding the word "agent."

MAJOR FOREIGN MARKETS

Although markets are available worldwide for both the exporter and importer, recent changes in the European and Asian markets are making these countries exciting and profitable ones to target.

European Community

The European Community (EC) is working to completely drop barriers among its member nations for movement of capital, goods, people and services. The united European market is the largest market in the world. The original EC member countries were:

Belgium	Denmark
France	Germany
Greece	Ireland
Italy	Luxembourg
The Netherlands	Portugal
Spain	United Kingdom

This multitrillion dollar market of some 360 million consumers is growing with the addition of new member countries that will bring the total of a more-or-less united market to almost half a billion customers, most of whom are fairly well off with substantial disposable income. (Germany alone has a gross domestic product of approximately $1.6 trillion per year and is the world's largest international trader.)

If you visit any of these countries, you will see T-shirts with names of U.S. rock groups and football teams, western turquoise jewelry on sale in the shops, and blue jeans on Europe's youth. American culture's popularity in the EC provides you with great sales opportunities.

Where the people are not well off, the countries have definite modernization programs underway that need not only raw materials but also the latest technology.

As an exporter, you no longer need a distributor in each country. With the elimination of trade barriers, a distributor in any of these countries can import your products and then resell to any of the other countries without tariffs, export declarations or other barriers. A German company distributing U.S. products to Europe is in a very similar situation to a New Jersey company distributing German products to all fifty states. Just make sure you find a good distributor with contacts throughout Europe.

The U.S. Department of Commerce maintains staff to help you sell to the EC and other European nations. Contact the European Market Information Service, U.S. Department of Commerce, Room 3036, 14th & Constitution Avenue, NW, Washington, DC 20230, (202) 482-5823.

Breaking Into the Japanese Market

Trade with Japan is frequently in the headlines. I have deliberately used Japan as an export example many times in this book to communicate the idea that you *can* export to Japan. It is important to investigate selling to Japan. Currently, their economy is estimated as having a gross domestic product of approximately $3.4 trillion per year (compared to our $6.7 trillion per year).

It is true that exporting to Japan is difficult if you have a product that is manufactured domestically in Japan. But other than that, the market is truly as open to you as to anyone.

A number of books deal specifically with trading with Japan. The Japan External Trade Organization, or JETRO (see Resource List), has some excellent tapes available, and many colleges and universities run seminars on exporting to Japan.

There are three keys to doing a successful business with Japan: Sell through an established distributor for your industry, be meticulous about the quality of your product, and commit to the business as a long-term relationship. These three points are, of course, highly abbreviated concepts. But I believe these are the three most important points. If you stick to them you will not go wrong, and you have enough information to get started.

Selling Through an Established Distributor

The Japanese distribution system has grown up over the years, based on loyalty in a long chain of distribution. Each company purchases from a specific supplier out of a loyalty that may go back generations.

Mr. Yokamura buys from Mr. Nishioka because Mr. Yokamura's grandfather bought from Mr. Nishioka's grandfather. There is no question of going to a new vendor. So if you want your goods in Mr. Yokamura's place of business, you must sell your goods to Mr. Nishioka's firm. If you tried to sell directly to Mr. Yokamura, he would not buy your product no matter how good it is because he buys only from Mr. Nishioka.

Likewise, you cannot sell to Mr. Nishioka if he buys your type of product only from Mr. Keisanata. You must find a national company that distributes through this network, and sell to them. (JETRO can supply you with lists.)

This seems like an extremely complicated way to do things. But remember ethnocentrism? This is the way Japanese businesses operate *now*. It will probably change in the years to come. If you want to sell to Japan now, you must accept things the way they are now.

Committing to Quality

Japanese consumers are used to top-quality goods and services, and this means defect-free goods. This expectation is built into the culture.

A few years ago, the compressor went out on my car's air conditioner. I live in Phoenix and it was August, so I couldn't live without it. I took it to a local company that specializes in car air conditioners. They kept the car for three days and when I picked it up, that car was like a refrigerator. (For $650.00, it should have been!)

About two weeks later, the air conditioner failed again. I brought it back in, and the manager was most apologetic and promised to have it taken care of right away. There was a ninety-day warranty on the work.

I came back for the car at the end of the day and it was like a refrigerator again! And it has been working that way for over three years.

As Americans, our attitude is usually, "It should have been done right the first time!" And so it should have.

But if this had happened in Japan: (1) The manager and his family would have lost face in the community. (2) All the workers for the repair shop would have lost face, even if they had not been involved in the repair. (3) All their families would have lost face. (4) Anyone working for the car manufacturer who heard about my problem would have lost face in the community—because the original equipment should have lasted longer.

This is part of the culture: If it is not right, if it is not perfect, one loses face and is shamed before the community. So, if you sell to a Japanese distributor and your product is second rate, does not work or breaks down, the distributor will lose face in front of the entire community and bring shame on his family.

This is a very serious part of the Japanese makeup, and who is to say it is wrong? It has not only brought about top-quality manufacturing in Japan but also a need for exporters to Japan to deliver nothing less than top quality.

If you can produce top-quality products, *and* if you are not competing with a Japanese domestic manufacturer, you can sell to a distributor in Japan.

Building Long-Term Relationships

Be in for the long term. The Japanese way of doing business is to build up a business relationship that will last for many years. Remember Mr. Yokamura and Mr. Nishioka? Their business relationship began with their grandfathers' business relationship, and this is all seen as quite normal.

If you plan to sell to Japan, think in terms not of the profit to be made in the next calendar quarter, but in terms of the profit to be made over the next two or three generations. Anything less is seen by the Japanese as being "short term," and it is not attractive to them.

Selling to China

China's market of more than one billion people is beginning to turn into a consuming nation. The country still needs to purchase technology that it cannot make at home—everything from machine tools to chemical compounds. But the consumer market is growing, too.

About ten years ago, the concept developed of the "Eight Bigs" that every Chinese family was to strive to own: television, refrigerator, stereo, camera, motorcycle, furniture, washing machine and electric fan. These are very modest material goals to most Americans but from a business point of view, think of a market of one billion consumers, many of whom are striving to own the "Eight Bigs."

Many successful Chinese entrepreneurs have long since secured the "Eight Bigs" and are now enthusiastically pursuing goals of more expensive and elaborate possessions, as well as increased profits from their business ventures.

Setting up a business presence in China can be very complex. As a starting point, you may want to sell to a Hong Kong wholesale firm with contacts in China. Your first step is to contact the Hong Kong Trade Development Council (see Resource List).

For years Hong Kong merchants have been buying and selling between China and the rest of the world and have been the "back door" to China trade. During the years when China substantially shut itself off from the rest of the world with the Bamboo Curtain, Hong Kong was the only outlet for Chinese goods and the only way for foreign goods to enter. As trade has increased, the established merchants of Hong Kong, with contacts throughout China, have been in an ideal position to be the export trading companies for both sides.

Hong Kong is scheduled to become part of mainland China in 1997 but to retain its capitalist economy. Going through Hong Kong remains your best means of entering the massive Chinese market or of obtaining Chinese goods for import.

Emerging Asian Markets

Taiwan, Singapore, Hong Kong and South Korea have been nicknamed the "Four Tigers" as countries that are developing very rapidly. They are markets for technology, raw materials, and, since their people are affluent and growing more so, consumer goods. They are among our major trading partners and are countries you should be interested in targeting.

The next generation is coming along: In Indonesia, Malaysia, the Philippines and Thailand the industry of the Four Tigers, and Japanese industry are establishing offshore manufacturing. Consumers in these countries will be hungrily looking for new consumer goods over the next ten years.

COMMITTING FOR THE LONG TERM

International trade is not a quick-in, quick-out endeavor. For a company to be truly profitable in exporting or importing, it and its employees must make a long-term commitment to the business.

Balancing Domestic Sales

Sometimes a company becomes involved in international sales because domestic sales are down. This is a viable way of evening out the business cycle and extending a product's life cycle. Many of the most profitable companies in the world, large and small, become involved in export for this reason.

Sometimes management is tempted to back off from exporting when domestic sales pick up. This can be a costly mistake for two reasons:

1. The U.S. economy is such a powerful force that when the U.S. economy picks up, it tends to spark the rest of the world's economy. So when your U.S. sales pick up, international sales

should increase the same time.

2. If you work to establish international sales during a depressed period, your work may just be ready to pay off handsomely months later—when your domestic business picks up again.

So if you are considering international trade to help make a profit when business has been slow, keep your commitment when business improves. Things can only get better for you internationally.

Allow Plenty of Start-Up Time

It is not uncommon for a company to start off enthusiastically embracing the idea of international trade, and put in a significant amount of time and effort, only to drop it entirely before a profit is ever made. You must make the following commitments:

You must be committed for the long haul, not for the next quarter. It is easy to underestimate the time involved in putting together the first transaction. A year of correspondence and negotiation may pass between an inquiry and the day you actually ship to that company under a letter of credit. Or it may take less time. But the commitment must be there so that when it takes time and effort, you will give it the time and effort needed. Once the products are on the shelves, reorders can move faster.

Similarly, you may contact and be contacted by a hundred companies before finding exactly the right mix that will make for a good, mutually profitable relationship for many years to come. Realize from the beginning that not everyone you contact will be a profitable customer or supplier.

Make the Commitment Company Wide

Middle management and employees must understand the company's commitment to international trade over a long period of time and the eventual benefits to all. Make clear that job security, overtime and other benefits may not happen right away, but as the company succeeds, all succeed.

All levels of the company must not only agree to the plan to expand internationally but understand what will be required of them. Likewise, management must understand what will be required by each part of the company for the project's success. A twofold Japanese concept illustrates this:

1. First, the *nemawashi*. This is the process of management in approaching all departments with its new idea, explaining its value and asking for input.
2. Second, the *ringisho*. This is an actual document, like a business plan, that is passed around to the heads of the departments involved, outlining the master plan, what is required of each department, and what support each department will be provided. The department heads approve the *ringisho*, and when top management proceeds to implement the plan, everyone is both committed to the project and knows exactly what is to be done.

In entering international trade, the *nemawashi* and *ringisho* concepts can be implemented in the very beginning to obtain an overall commitment from the company with a general plan. Later, as specific orders come up, the concept can be used again so that everyone knows what is expected and the international orders flow through the company's system smoothly.

YOUR ENTRANCE INTO INTERNATIONAL TRADE

In the beginning of this book, I told you that the firm that isn't thinking in terms of international trade should be thinking of going out of business. By virtue of having read this book, you have equipped yourself to gain entry to the limitless possibilities that international business offers.

- You have learned the concepts.
- You have learned the terminology.
- You have learned where to go for help.
- You have learned how vital it is to participate in a global economy.

With the information you have now, you should be able to make a strong start in the exciting and profitable expansion of your business. When you need more information, you will know where to get it. You know the pitfalls to avoid, and you know how to go about international business profitably.

This gives you all the tools you need to go from here.

Make it happen.

ABI (Automated Broker Interface): A computer system that allows a Customs Broker to interface directly with U.S. Customs' computer system.

Advising bank: Bank that advises an exporter of a letter of credit.

AGR imports: American goods returned.

All-in: A freight quotation including all charges, often in one lump sum rather than broken down.

Amendment: A proposed change to a letter of credit.

Applicant: Party opening a letter of credit (importer).

Banker's acceptance: Importer's bank accepts responsibility to pay against a draft (substituting for the importer's responsibility).

Beneficiary: Party to be paid under a letter of credit (exporter).

Bill of lading: Contract of carriage between shipper (exporter) and carrier (steamship line, NVOCC, airline, railroad or trucking company).

BSC (Bunker Surcharge): An extra charge by the carrier to adjust for temporarily higher fuel costs. Also called *fuel surcharge*.

Bunker Surcharge: *See* BSC.

CAF (Currency Adjustment Factor): Additional charge in carrier's tariff when the currency used for payment is valued low in relation to other currencies.

Cargo NES or Cargo NOS (Cargo Not Elsewhere Specified or Cargo Not Otherwise Specified): Carrier's tariff description for items not specifically listed in the tariff. Usually the highest rate.

Carnet: A document obtained by a Customs Broker to enable goods to travel through several countries without paying duty, then to be returned intact to the country of origin.

CFR (Cost and Freight) named point: The exporter's price includes the cost of the merchandise and all shipping costs to the named point. Also called $C+F$ and *C&F*.

CFS (Container Freight Station): Where less-than-container-load ocean shipments are brought to be loaded into a container (export) or unloaded from containers and made available for customs clearance (import).

CIF (Cost, Insurance and Freight) named point: The exporter's price includes the cost of the merchandise, all shipping costs to the named point and insurance.

CIP (Carriage and Insurance Paid) named point: The exporter's price includes the cost of the merchandise, all shipping costs to the named point (inland city) and insurance.

Confirming bank: A bank in the exporter's country that stands behind payment of a letter of credit when documents are presented in a timely manner and without discrepancies. Usually the advising bank.

Consolidation: An air freight forwarder's system of combining many small shipments into one large shipment on a scheduled aircraft. (Slang: "Consol.")

Consularization: Approval of export documents by a foreign consulate or other entity in the United States.

Consumption entry: A type of customs entry admitting goods into the commerce of the United States. May be formal or informal.

Correspondent: A bank, Customs Broker, freight forwarder, etc., working with others in another city or country to expedite transactions.

CPT (Carriage Paid To) named point: The exporter's price includes the cost of the merchandise and all shipping costs to a named inland point (beyond the ocean port).

Customs Broker: An individual or a firm licensed by the government to undertake customs clearance and other services for the importing public.

CY (container yard): Where ocean containers are received, stored, and made available for delivery.

DAF (Delivered At Frontier) named point: The exporter's price includes the cost of the merchandise and all shipping costs to the named point at the border.

DDC (Destination Delivery Charges): Unloading charges at destination port of a steamship line or NVOCC.

Discrepancy: A document, or part of a document, that does not exactly conform to a letter of credit.

EC (European Community): The customs union of countries in Europe, organizing freedom of movement for goods, services, capital and people.

Ethnocentrism: A belief that the way things are done in a particular person's culture is automatically the correct way for everyone. Anyone who deviates is doing wrong.

Export Management Company: A company that sells products abroad for another company, and ordinarily arranges the transportation and financial transactions, usually on a commission basis.

Export Trading Company: A company that takes title to goods and then resells them.

EXW (Ex Works) named point: The exporter's price includes making the goods available at the named point (his "works"), ready for shipment.

FAK (Freight, All Kinds): Carrier's tariff description including any and all kinds of freight under this category, all at one rate regardless of density, value, etc.

FAS (Free Alongside Ship) named point: The exporter's price includes the cost of the merchandise and all shipping costs to the vessel at the named port.

FCA (Free Carrier) named point: The exporter's price includes making the goods available at the named point (his "works") and loading the shipment.

FCL (Full Container Load): Usually refers to ocean shipments.

FOB (Free on Board) carrier named point: The exporter's price includes the cost of the merchandise and all shipping costs to the named point, including loading on board the carrier and forwarder's fees. Applies to vessel, truck, train and air shipments.

Foreign trade zone: A specific place designated by U.S. Customs Service to be outside the customs territory of the United States, permitting duty-free storage, display and manipulation of imported goods.

Free trade agreement: An agreement between countries to reduce and eventually eliminate tariff and nontariff barriers between them.

Freight Forwarder: A travel agent for freight.

FSC (Fuel Surcharge): Additional charge in a carrier's tariffs when the price of fuel increases.

Gateway: A principal airport, domestic or international, with many flights, offering maximum service and connections. Sometimes used to refer to a truck or rail border crossing to Canada or Mexico.

Gross weight: The total weight of a shipment.

Interline service: A routing from origin to destination involving more than one carrier.

Intermodal: More than one mode of transportation is used, e.g., truck and steamship, in one shipment, and one bill of lading is issued for the entire shipment.

IT (In-transit) entry: A customs entry permitting goods to move between ports under bond.

Landbridge: A microbridge or a minibridge.

LCL (Less-Than-Container Load): Usually refers to ocean shipments.

Legalization: Approval of export documents by a foreign consulate or other entity in the United States.

Letter of credit: Letter issued by a bank to arrange payment for goods.

LTL: Less-Than-Truckload

M3: Cubic meters.

Microbridge: A rate from a city that is not a seaport to a foreign city, via another city that is a seaport, with the steamship line or NVOCC issuing a bill of lading from the original city and taking responsibility for the cargo all the way. Example: Phoenix to Tokyo via Los Angeles.

Minibridge: A rate from a city that is a seaport to a foreign seaport, via another city that is a seaport, with the steamship line or NVOCC issuing a bill of lading from the origin city and taking responsibility for the cargo all the way. Example: Los Angeles to Le Havre via Galveston.

Negotiable: A document that can be used to claim title to the cargo, as in a "negotiable instrument."

Net weight: The weight of the goods themselves, not counting packing materials.

Non-negotiable: A document that cannot be used to claim title to the cargo. Most important: Air waybills are always non-negotiable.

Non-tariff barrier: Any barrier to imports into a country. Official: boycott, inspection, licensing, quota. Nonofficial: custom, language, prejudice, style.

NVOCC (non-vessel operating common carrier): A company that issues its own bills of lading and rates using another company's vessels.

Opening bank: A bank that opens a letter of credit at the request of an importer.

Origin receiving charges: Loading charges at origin point. *See* TRC.

Pro forma invoice: A quotation to the buyer.

Sight draft: A draft payable upon acceptance by the buyer.

STC (Said to contain): Sometimes applied by a forwarder or a carrier to documents as part of the description of the goods, e.g., "10 cartons stc 1,000 textbooks."

Tare weight: The weight of the packing materials in a shipment (net plus tare equals gross weight).

Tariff: A schedule of rates published by a carrier. Also can refer to the Harmonized Tariff Schedule of the United States, which covers customs duties.

Tariff barrier: Customs duties, which are one possible barrier to imports into a country by making them more expensive.

TIB (Temporary Import under Bond): A procedure in which goods are imported without payment of duty, by posting a bond to guarantee that they will be exported.

Time draft: A draft payable at a discernible time after acceptance by the buyer, e.g., "30 days after sight."

TL: Truckload

Transship: To change carriers in a foreign port en route to a third port. Also used to refer to a country of transshipment, as: "We are shipping from Canada to Mexico, transshipping across the United States."

TRC (Terminal Receiving Charges): Loading charges at origin port of a steamship line or NVOCC.

VAT (Value Added Tax): A national sales tax on goods and/or services. Used in Europe and elsewhere.

Warehouse entry: A Customs Entry permitting goods to enter a bonded warehouse.

Warehouse withdrawal: A Customs Entry permitting goods to leave a bonded warehouse.

Wharfage: A fee for using a wharf or pier at the origin or destination point. Generally included under terminal receiving charges.

LEADS FOR EXPORTERS

American Export Register
Directory of U.S. Exporters
Thomas International Publishing Co.
1 Penn Plaza
250 West Thirty-fourth Street
New York, NY 10119

Exporter's Directory
Journal of Commerce
110 Wall Street
New York, NY 10005

International Directory of Importers
105 Dry Creek Road
Heraldsburg, CA 95448

DOCUMENTATION, LOGISTICS, AND PROCEDURES, FOR EXPORTERS

A Basic Guide to Exporting
U.S. Government Printing Office
Washington, DC 20402
   (Or contact your local office of the U.S.
   Department of Commerce, U.S. and
   Foreign Commercial Service.)

Export Documentation Handbook
Exporter's Encyclopedia
Dunn's Marketing Services
3 Entry Drive
Parsippany, NJ 07054

Official Export Guide
North American Publishing Company
401 North Broad Street
Philadelphia, PA 19108

CUSTOMS REGULATIONS AND TARIFFS (DUTY)

Customs Regulations of the United States
Harmonized Tariff Schedule of the United
States

Importing to the United States
U.S. Government Printing Office
Washington, DC 20402
   (Or contact the local office of the U.S.
   Customs Service.)

Incoterms 1990
ICC Publishing Corporation
156 Fifth Avenue, Suite 820
New York, NY 10010

U.S. Custom House Guide
North American Publishing Company
401 North Broad Street
Philadelphia, PA 19108

PUBLICATIONS FOR INTERNATIONAL BUSINESS

Eastern Europe Business Bulletin
U.S. Department of Commerce
Room 7412
Eastern Europe Business Information
Center
Washington, DC 20230

Journal of Commerce
110 Wall Street
New York, NY 10005
   (Newspaper, published business days.)

National Motor Freight Classification
2200 Mill Road
Alexandria, VA 22314

COMPUTER SOFTWARE

XDOC
Cascade Interactive Designs
1300 Spring Street
Seattle, Washington 98104-1348
(206) 720-1234
Fax: (206) 720-6211
   (To assist with export documentation.)

Unz & Company
190 Baldwin Avenue
Jersey City, NJ 07306
(800) 631-3098
In NJ: (201) 795-5400

TELEVISION PROGRAMS

Times vary. Check your local listings.

On PBS (Public Broadcasting Service): "Adam Smith's Money World" (an in-depth exploration of one business topic per week, either domestic or international)

On CNN (Cable News Network): "Inside Business" (an in-depth exploration of one business topic per week, either domestic or international), and "Moneyweek" (a collection of business stories from the week, either domestic or international)

In Syndication: "Wall Street Week" (summaries of selected business stories of the week)

FLASH FACTS

A service of the U.S. Department of Commerce to help with international trade with Canada, Mexico, and the independent states of the former Soviet Union.
Call from any touch-tone telephone and follow the instructions to receive a table of contents, or to obtain any report in the system. Enter your fax number and the information will be sent to you at no charge.

Canada Flash Facts:
(202) 482-3101
(dial 0100 for Table of Contents)

Mexico Flash Facts:
(202)482-4464
(dial 0100 for Table of Contents)

Newly Independent States Flash Facts:
(202) 482-3145
Tables of Contents

0001 for Trade and Investment Opportunities
0002 for industry-specific and country-specific information
0003 for list of periodical publications

EXPORT HOTLINE

Call (800) 896-1111 to register.
(Provides 4,500 trade leads and reports at no cost. You can post information on your own company for a nominal fee. The Export Hotline is sponsored by several large corporations in association with the U.S. Department of Commerce. Before using the Hotline, you must register your company.)

SPECIAL SERVICES

Language Line
AT&T
(800) 628-8486
(AT&T Language Line service puts an interpreter for any of 140 languages on the telephone line between you and your foreign-language customer. Available twenty-four hours a day.)

SBDC
Small Business Development Center
(Funded by the Small Business Administration; free resource centers for various aspects of business, including international trade: classes, consulting, reference library.)

SCORE
Service Corps of Retired Executives
Small Business Administration
(Retired executives from international trade and other fields available for free consultation.)

SUPPLY HOUSES SPECIALIZING IN INTERNATIONAL FORMS

Apperson Business Forms
8616 East Slauson Avenue
Pico Rivera, CA 90660
(800) 438-0162
In CA: (310) 949-4952

Unz & Company
190 Baldwin Avenue
Jersey City, NJ 07306
(800) 631-3098
In NJ: (201) 795-5400

INTERNATIONAL TRADE ORGANIZATIONS

Hong Kong Trade Development Council
Los Angeles World Trade Center
350 South Figueroa Street
Los Angeles, CA 90071-1306
(213) 622-3193
Fax: (213) 613-1490

Japan External Trade Organization
(JETRO)
1221 Avenue of the Americas
New York, NY 10020
(212) 302-1581
Fax: (212) 997-0464

World Trade Center Association
Headquarters
One World Trade Center, Suite 7701
New York, NY 10048
(212) 313-4600

INTERNATIONAL CARGO INSURANCE

The Roanoke Companies
1930 Thoreau Drive
Schaumburg, IL 60173
(800) 338-0753
In IL: (708) 490-9540

INDEX

More Great Books for Smart Decisions!

Doing Business in Asia: A Small Business Guide to Success in the World's Most Dynamic Market—For small and medium-sized American companies, this book offers the information, insights and encouragement needed to start doing business in Asia's principal markets.
#70198/$18.95/192 pages/paperback

Homemade Money, 5th Edition—You'll be up to speed on the legal matters, accounting practices, tax laws, and marketing techniques sure to make your home-based business a success!
#70231/$19.99/400 pages/paperback

How to Run a Family Business—To ensure your family business stays afloat, you need sound advice. You'll find everything you need to know, from forming a board of directors, to setting salaries in this indispensable resource.
#70214/$14.95/176 pages/paperback

Becoming Financially Sound in an Unsound World—In this strategic guide, you'll find financial security while improving your personal well-being with a positive outlook.
#70140/$14.95/240 pages/paperback

Cleaning Up for a Living—Learn from the best! Don Aslett shares with you the tricks and tips he used to build a $12 million commercial cleaning business.
#70016/$12.95/208 pages/paperback

Success, Common Sense, and the Small Business—As a small business owner, you need to wear a lot of hats. This information-packed guide covers the skills required when one person is responsible for a variety of tasks. *#70212/$11.95/176 pages/paperback*

How to Make $100,000 a Year Desk-Top Publishing—Get the inside details on this ever-growing industry. You'll discover how to begin a project and see it through to completion. Plus get information on every type of publication.
#70054/$18.95/280 pages/paperback

Rehab Your Way to Riches—Let a real estate mogul in control of $4 million in assets show you how to generate real estate income in ways that limit risk and maximize profits.
#70156/$14.95/208 pages/paperback

The Complete Guide to Contracting Your Home—This all-in-one guide covers everything from site selection to financing your new home. Plus, you'll get a crash-course on dealing with suppliers, subcontractors, building inspectors, and more!
#70025/$18.99/288 pages/paperback

How To Have a Great Retirement on a Limited Budget—Make your Golden Years truly golden. Here are dozens of practical, proven ways to enjoy a fun, full life when you retire.
#10288/$12.95/145 pages/paperback

Legal Aspects of Buying, Owning, & Selling a Home—In this easy-to-read guide you'll find the answers to all your legal questions concerning buying, selling, and occupying a home.
#70151/$12.95/176 pages/paperback

The Consumer's Guide to Understanding and Using the Law—Practical advice—not legal mumbo-jumbo—will teach you your rights in family law, real estate, criminal law and more!
#70236/$14.99/288 pages/paperback

Mortgage Loans: What's Right for You?—Don't make a big-money mistake signing for the wrong mortgage! Find the facts on the types of mortgages perfectly suited to your needs and financial situation. Plus get information on caps, margins, points, and more!
#70242/$14.95/144 pages/paperback

Home Buyer's Inspection Guide—Don't get caught in a money-pit! Let an expert building inspector teach you all the critical structural and functional aspects of residential property—before you buy.
#70049/$12.99/176 pages/paperback

The Complete Guide to Buying Your First Home—This information-packed guide shows you how to plan and organize your buy, and how to avoid common pitfalls for first-time home buyers.
#70023/$16.99/224 pages/paperback

The Single Person's Guide to Buying A Home—This buying guide offers you worksheets and checklists that show you what to look for when buying a home on your own.
#70200/$14.95/144 pages/paperback

Raising Happy Kids on a Reasonable Budget—As seen on Oprah Winfrey, this one-of-a-kind guide is packed with dollar-stretching techniques and budgeting tips you need to raise happy and healthy kids—whether you have one child or ten!
#70184/$10.95/144 pages/paperback

Kids, Money & Values—Packed with activities, games, and projects! You'll have a lot of fun as you teach your kids good money management habits!
#70238/$10.99/144 pages/paperback

The Organization Map—You WILL defeat disorganization. This effective guide is chock full of tips for time-management, storage solutions and more!
#70224/$12.95/208 pages/paperback

Conquering The Paper Pile-Up—You'll find the right place to file and store every piece of paper in your home and office.
#10178/$11.95/176 pages/paperback

Slow Down and Get More Done—Determine the right pace for your life by gaining control of worry, making possibilities instead of plans, and learning the value of doing "nothing."
#70183/$11.95/192 pages/paperback

Collecting Paper Money for Pleasure and Profit—Whether you're a beginning or veteran collector or investor, you'll be fascinated by this comprehensive guide!
#70143/$18.95/240 pages/paperback

Collecting Coins for Pleasure and Profit—Discover tips on preserving, buying and selling coins; the history of U.S. coins; and information on numismatic periodicals, national coin societies and more!
#70018/$18.95/224 pages/paperback

The Inventor's Handbook: How to Develop, Protect, & Market Your Invention, 2nd Edition—Provides practicing and prospective inventors with the tools to take their ideas from concept to production to marketing. *#70062/$14.95/232 pages/paperback*

Cover Letters That Will Get You the Job You Want—Shows how to introduce yourself and your resume compellingly and efficiently with a well-written, well constructed cover letter. Includes 100 tested cover letters that work!
#70185/$12.99/192 pages/paperback

The Edge Resume & Job Search Strategy—Job Hunters—learn to create the kind of resumes that will stand out in a stack—and use them to open the right doors.
#70298/$23.95/172 pages/paperback

Making the Most of the Temporary Employment Market—In an age of corporate downsizing, get up to speed on the benefits of temporary work.
#70197/$9.95/176 pages/paperback

Write to the address below for a FREE catalog of all Betterway Books. To order books directly from the publisher, include $3.50 postage and handling for one book, $1.00 for each additional book. Ohio residents add 5½% sales tax. Allow 30 days for delivery.

Betterway Books
1507 Dana Avenue
Cincinnati, Ohio 45207

VISA/MasterCard orders call TOLL-FREE
1-800-289-0963

Prices subject to change without notice.   Stock may be limited on some books.

Write to this address for a catalog of Betterway Books, plus information on *Writer's Digest* magazine, *Story* magazine, Writer's Digest Book Club, Writer's Digest School, and Writer's Digest Criticism Service.   3131